John & Sandy,

What an absolutely
incredible time I had
with you both. Thanks
for sharing your heart
with me Sunday &

Love
Debbie

John 8

Freeing the Prisoner From Within

Crush the Chains Choking Your Destiny

Debbie Ormonde, DDiv

ISBN 9780578458700

Foreword

I have known Debbie and her husband, Kevin, for many years. I watched them grow in their walk with the Lord, get married, and serve Him together. This book tells the story of how God turned a life of pain, disappointment, and tragedy into an incredible testimony of healing and forgiveness that has ministered to thousands of people. Debbie's book is a powerful testimony of what the Lord can do in an individual's life when they learn how to fully surrender to Him. I pray that, as you read this book, you will be challenged to surrender more and more of your life to Him and experience the freeing of the prisoner within you.

—Jeff Johnson
Sr. Pastor, Calvary Chapel
Downey, CA

Contents

Part One

Chapter 1

The Prize

"Do you not know that in a race all the runners run,
but only one gets the prize? Run in such a way as to get the prize."
— 1 Corinthians 9:24 (NIV)

Waiting for the bus that day with the warmth of the summer sun on my face, it was easy to get lost in a place of hope. To breathe in fresh air ... dance like no one was watching ... and channel all of my emotions into being alive. Disappointments didn't hurt so much that I couldn't bounce back. Hearing the word "no" didn't mean never, and I could see a future so great that no one else could even imagine it. But I had no idea where life was about to take me.

Standing at the bus stop near my childhood home that Sunday morning, I waited patiently for the same white church bus that had come to get me so many times before. Although I stood alone, I felt safe and secure, knowing I was on my way to an extraordinary day. As we pulled up to church, I could hardly contain my anticipation. I jumped off the bus and ran straight to my classroom, eager to see the award I'd worked so hard all summer to earn by memorizing countless Bible verses.

Quickly, I scanned the room until my eyes locked onto my teacher's desk. There it was! A blue leather-bound Bible with my name, Debbie Acorn, engraved resplendently in gold. It was destined to become my most prized possession.

I'd felt a special love for the Bible since attending Vacation Bible School the year before and surrendering my heart to the loving leadership of Jesus Christ. Today, I could hardly wait to get home and travel back in time by reading the stories held between the pages of my leather-bound treasure. Something about reading the Bible deeply intrigued me. Even at age 9, I understood what I was reading and my appetite for learning seemed insatiable. For the first time, I felt connected to something permanent, immense, and important, and I was not going to let that connection go.

It was the beginning of a relationship that would sustain me over the next 35 years, even as I traveled through heartache and hell to learn the most important lesson of my life: Sometimes, freedom means freeing the prisoner from within.

Chapter 2

That's B.S.: Brother Sprinkles

*"When you stop chasing the right things, you give
the wrong things a chance to catch you."*
– Debbie Ormonde

It was 1969, the year of peace, love, Jesus freaks, the Vietnam war, sit-ins, and protests. It was also the year that Brother Jigg Sprinkles entered my life. Some people described him as a charismatic ministry leader, so compassionate that he'd literally give you the shirt off of his back. Others saw him as a calculating and disingenuous egomaniac who was eager to exert cult-like control over his growing group of followers. My parents were in the former group. I was in the latter. And what started as a mere difference of opinions eventually led to my complete undoing.

My Uncle Luther, a valiant Korean War Purple Heart recipient, introduced our family to Brother Sprinkles, whose initials ironically provide an apt description of his *modus operandi*. My wheelchair-bound uncle's bottomless wellspring of joy revealed a deep love for Jesus that, no doubt, tempted many an able-bodied Christian to want to trade places with him. My mom's older brother, Uncle Luther spent countless hours ministering to my parents and was instrumental in their decision to trust Jesus as their Savior. Soon afterward, he invited us to attend his church, where Brother Sprinkles was the co-pastor. Unfortunately for me, this ended my bus rides to the church I'd been attending by myself for the past year and brought me into frequent contact with the man who would soon become my archnemesis.

~

Why would God allow an evil enemy to convince the woman I love—the woman whose job it is to love, protect, and nurture me—to hurt me like this? There was no answer, only silence.

~

I was dumbfounded that my parents couldn't see what I saw in "B.S.," as I came to think of him. After all, I'd attended church before they did. I'd sought a relationship with God before they did. Why did they so easily dismiss my intuition about this slick, so-called man of God when I could see right through him? Unable to sway them, I watched, repulsed, as he convinced my parents they could have everything they wanted simply by following him. Like impressionable sheep, they believed everything Brother Sprinkles said ... and acted on it, too.

My parents publicly professed their new-found faith in Jesus Christ at the pulpit during services jointly led by Brother Sprinkles and the church's senior pastor, Brother Caewood. Now *there* was a man I could sincerely call "brother." Big and burly, Brother Caewood was a thoughtful, gracious man whose charisma intrigued people and inspired action. I'm not sure exactly how these two "brothers" got mixed up together, but apparently their co-leadership roles didn't last long. A church split ensued, with half the congregation backing Brother Caewood and the other half solidly supporting Brother Sprinkles.

Naturally, I backed Brother Caewood, as did Uncle Luther. My parents, however, couldn't see beyond Brother Sprinkles' confident exterior to detect the legalistic, prideful, graceless core that lurked within. I resented the days we were forced to attend services with Brother Sprinkles. The more we attended, the more involved my parents became in his church and the closer they got to him. My happy little bubble was shrinking day by day ... with me inside! I could feel mounting tension, anger, and resentment taking root in my heart. And then the unthinkable happened.

One night, like many nights before, Brother Sprinkles was visiting with my parents in our home. Overhearing them talking, I still remember the exchange as if it were yesterday. In a grave tone befitting a funeral service, Brother Sprinkles told my mother that the only Bible Christians should read is the "authorized" King James version. Period. Harboring (much less reading) any other translation in our home would be an affront to the Creator and bring condemnation upon my parents and me. As if hypnotized, my mother dutifully embraced the edict as my father looked on in silence, no questions asked. Up until then, my mother clearly had worn the pants in our household, but not after Brother Sprinkles showed up. Now, there was a new sheriff in town and his instructions and biblical interpretations were the law.

So, when Brother Sprinkles pronounced that my prized, blue, leather-bound, gold-name-engraved Bible must immediately be replaced by the only acceptable translation, my heart sank. A lump formed in my throat and my eyes filled with tears. Seized by fear and disbelief, my mind raced, searching for a way to convince my mom to spare my prized possession. But my anxiety and sadness didn't seem to matter anymore. Later that evening, my mother uttered five words that shattered my heart: "That Bible has to go."

Feeling betrayed, my heart filled with a hatred toward Brother Sprinkles that I'd never felt toward anyone. I spent many nights after that in tears, crying out to no one in particular, *Why would God let this happen? If He's good, if He's loving, why would He allow an evil enemy to convince the woman I love—the woman whose job it is to love, protect, and nurture me—to hurt me like this?* There was no answer, only silence.

Over the next several years, I worked hard to numb my growing sense of bitterness, betrayal, and pain. My parents, meanwhile, continued to force my older brother, Steven, and me to attend B.S.'s sad excuse for a church, though it wasn't a viable way to meet my spiritual needs.

Though I remember little about Steven's life before this pivotal period, I do recall being suddenly intrigued by his rebellious lifestyle, which led me to spend more and more time with him. Steven helped me learn how to bypass the rules at home and school so I could live life on my own terms. From now on, I told myself, I would let no one steal from my heart again. *This heart was closed for business.*

Gradually, the hopeful eyes of a child became the jaded eyes of disappointment as I sought ways to distract myself from my broken heart. Doing what was fun, and anything that would keep me far away from Brother Sprinkles, was my new agenda. I was 10 years old and focused single-mindedly on one thing: the party life.

My brother was getting in trouble with the law often and, at age 16, he was sentenced to prison. While there, my parents were going through their own troubles and my dad moved out. At that point, my mom—in an incredible about-face—started hanging out with drug dealers. (Where Brother Sprinkles was during this family crisis, I don't know.) Perhaps my mother didn't realize the damaging influence her new friends were having on her, but I remember coming home one day and finding her drinking and getting high. Suddenly, the version of the Bible that occupied our shelves seemed like the least of our problems.

Looking back, I believe that, as my mother watched my brother spiral downward, she adopted an "If you can't beat em', join em'" mentality. And right before my bewildered eyes, she morphed from "newly converted religious dictator" to "cool parent" and was sucked into a life of parties, drugs, alcohol, theft, and lying. Our home soon became the neighborhood safe house, a haven for anyone skipping school, running away, or fighting with their family. We harbored troubled kids, lied for them, and helped them live the party life they wanted.

One day, while Mom and a friend were out partying, I discovered her friend's car keys at my house and interpreted the oversight as an unmistakable invitation to take the car for a joyride. I drove 10 miles to pick up my best friend, Reggie, passing a reservoir in a wooded area along the way. When I arrived at Reggie's house, he looked at me and then the car and said, "No way am I getting in there with you!" Undaunted, I left and drove around some more. Eventually, I made it home safely—my escapade unnoticed by my mom or her friend. The outing marked a turning point for me, underscoring how much I loved the freedom that rebellion brought.

My Journey

A Start Here
T.O.D. (The Other Debbie)
1-14-2
trip in numerical order

♡ found out Emma was sick, Bellflower events, Taco Bell, St. Francis Hospital
D.I.W. (Debbie in Woods) Debbie ran through the woods to find Dad

🕯 Glass bottle cut eye

🍀 neice murdered in Indiana
🔥 River Rafting in Idaho

👪 family events

1. Virginia
2. North Carolina
3. West Virginia
4. Ohio
5. Indiana
6. Michigan
7. Illinois
8. Iowa
9. South Dakota
10. Montana
11. Idaho
12. Washington
13. Oregon
14. California

Chapter 3

On the Run

"Damaged people are dangerous; they know they can survive."
– Josephine Hart

I didn't realize when I said goodbye to my best friend, Reggie, and walked out of school one day several months after my first joyride, that it would be my last day at any school throughout my childhood. I had just started seventh grade, but the "substance of things hoped for"[1] had nothing to do with religion and everything to do with abusing substances and a preoccupation with sex and rock-n-roll. There were no rules or boundaries, and there was nothing to lose.

Heading home from school that day, I could see our brick house in the distance. Situated in the middle of a quiet, mature subdivision close to the woods, it had three bedrooms and was nicely decorated. As I approached, I saw a police car in the driveway, which was uncommon for our neighborhood. A police officer stood just inside our front door. *Something has gone down with my brother again*, I thought.

---

[1] Hebrews 11:1

But shortly after entering our home, I learned the officer wasn't there for Steven. He was waiting to arrest me.

This wasn't the first time I'd been picked up for truancy so I thought it would end uneventfully, like all the other times. *I'll be home in time for my favorite TV show,* I assured myself. But, this time, we didn't go to the police station. I was taken, instead, to Mecklenburg juvenile detention facility. As I walked through the doors, my demeanor became as hardened as the benches that lined the walls. Inside, though, I was trembling with fear. It was late at night, so the entrance was dark. Alone inside a cold, grey room furnished with only a bed, I cried myself to sleep.

A week later, I was standing before a judge who ruled that my parents were unfit to continue raising me. The hollow thud of a gavel made it official: I was a "ward of the state." I had no idea what those words meant, but then transferred to Bon Air Juvenile Detention Center. What I believed was a simple truancy issue turned out to be an "addicted-mother-arrested-for-welfare-fraud" issue, which left me living in a detention center. My heart felt shattered as I went to my desolate room that day. I longed to be home with my parents and brother—without rules, and in my own familiar space. However, my wishes were inconsequential to the state of Virginia.

Truancy officials had placed me in foster care twice before, but this was my first time being arrested and taken to a juvenile detention center. I thought about the foster system and the families I'd stayed with for just a few short weeks at a time. I ran away from the first home and barely remember the family. What I'll never forget, though, is the utter shock of being placed in someone else's home.

My second foster home left a more distinct impression. I was there for around a month before sneaking out a window and running away. It was a Christian family with five kids of their own. Each evening, they would sing Christian songs and play spiritual music before sitting down for dinner, and I remember being freaked out. Even so, being there was way better than the detention center where I now found myself. I remembered this second foster family singing the old gospel song, "Jesus Met the Woman at the Well," based on a Bible story I'd either forgotten or had never read. In the story, Jesus met an outcast woman as she was drawing water and He told her everything she'd ever done. As the five kids and their parents belted out, "You've got five husbands, and the one you have now, he's not your own," I struggled to figure out the song's meaning. One thing seemed clear: Jesus was nice to this woman, despite her troubled past. *If he loved her,* I reasoned, *he certainly could love me.* As my faint memories of foster homes faded, my mind returned to my present surroundings—the detention center, from which I had to find a new way to escape and return home. This time would not be as easy.

~

I respected and even admired him, but I didn't want to hear any preaching.

~

I lived at the detention center for about three months and, during that time, Brother Caewood visited me. While part of me was glad to see him, another part instantly recoiled, certain that he'd come to preach at me. I respected and even admired him, but I didn't want to hear any preaching.

The pastor sat down and asked how I was doing. After a bit more small talk, he asked, "Do you smoke?" Surprised by the randomness of his question, I responded with a resounding "Yes!" anticipating a lecture on the dangers of smoking. Instead, he asked, "Have you ever watched someone smoke?" With that, he began imitating a smoker, taking long drags and forming imaginary smoke rings with each exhale. The sight was comical—he looked ridiculous!—and we both laughed, dispelling the tension I'd felt when he first arrived. Then, he flicked the invisible cigarette away.

I was stunned that he wasn't trying to change or judge me; instead, he was simply loving me right where I was. He didn't spend a lot of time with me that day, but the genuine concern he showed by connecting and listening planted seeds and affected my life for many years to come. I'd never met anyone as genuinely caring. This 15-minute visit was one of the most impactful events of my life, speaking to my heart a message of God's unconditional love and acceptance.

Shortly after Brother Caewood's visit, I checked out a book from the juvenile facility's library: *The Cross and the Switchblade*, by David Wilkerson. Halfway through reading it, my mind was blown by the interactions between Nicky Cruz, the head of a ruthless New York gang, and Rev. Wilkerson, a Christian minister. As I read, I vividly envisioned each anecdote as if I were Nicky, including this one:

"You come near me and I'll kill you," Nicky warned.

"Yeah, you could do that," Rev. Wilkerson calmly replied. "You could cut me up into a thousand pieces and lay them in the street, and every piece will still love you."

When I read this, I was blown away that Rev. Wilkerson would risk his life to show the love of God to a hardened gangster who was threatening to kill him. *If God could love Nicky Cruz so much*, I mused, *maybe God might love me, too*.

As deeply as *The Cross and the Switchblade* affected me, it didn't persuade me to stay at Bon Air and, before long, I'd somehow managed to escape and return home. But that didn't last long. I was apprehended again and, this time, taken to a new detention facility—the Janie Porter Barrettt School for Girls. I was there for about four or five months before I escaped and called my dad to pick me up, which he did.

My father couldn't take me home for fear of being re-arrested, so my parents connected me with family friends. I stayed with them in Richmond, Virginia's "fan district," which got its name because the streets are arrayed like a fan. It was an artsy area, very cultured, with a lot of hippies. Jerry Lee Lewis was the main attraction at my first-ever concert in the park, which was located near the home where I was staying. Richmond was a college town and concert-goers were, predictably, drinking, smoking, and getting high. Soon the revelers began throwing glass bottles up in the air and, as I looked on, one careened down from the sky and hit me in the face, slicing a big gash underneath my right eye. My wound needed cleansing and stitches, but I didn't dare go to the hospital. I was afraid of being caught. Though I remained swollen and bruised for weeks, fortunately, my eye eventually healed. Even so, I still have a scar to remind me of that night.

After leaving Richmond, I flitted from place to place, staying with different friends of my parents, before finally moving back home. There, one evening, hanging out and listening to music with my brother and friends in the living room, the doorbell rang. Someone peeked through the curtains and announced the police were there. I knew I had to run and hide. A return trip to Janie Porter Barrett wasn't on my to do list. I fled to the attic and crouched on the floor as the others collapsed the stairs and closed the door behind me. My pulse racing, I listened in terror and disbelief as my brother's friend began singing "Folsom Prison Blues" by Johnny Cash. "I hear the train a coming…." Silence. And then I heard, "She's in the attic." *No!* I screamed within. *They're coming for me.* A police officer commanded me to come down. As I headed out the door to the squad car, I could still hear my brother's friend mocking me in song.

25

~

Undaunted, we pressed on, far more afraid of being caught than of running through the disorienting woods.

~

This time, a week of solitary confinement awaited me upon my return to Janie Porter Barrett. At 12 years old, I couldn't see or talk to anyone. I was incarcerated for less than a month before I escaped again, this time, never to return. I'd phoned my dad several times while I was detained and, during one of our conversations, we planned my escape. My dad was a strait-laced man who lived the life of an assembly-line foreman—sucked into an existence of non-stop work. We selected a date, time, and place to rendezvous upon my break from the Center. Frightened, I encouraged a friend, also named Debbie, to join my flight to freedom.

The day we escaped, we took off into the woods together before sunrise. Wearing shorts, I ran through the dark woods, scraping my legs on the brush though barely noticing it as fear fueled my adrenaline. Undaunted, we pressed on, far more afraid of being caught than of running through the disorienting woods. We had no idea where we were going and couldn't see anything or anyone. Finally, exhausted, we sat and waited for what seemed like hours … until we heard a man's voice. I was unsure at first of whose voice it was; but the second time, I knew it was the voice of my daddy. I jumped into his arms, and he hugged me tightly. At last, I felt relieved and safe.

My dad was shocked that I'd brought a friend with me, and from that moment on Debbie turned out to be a big problem for my parents. Even so, we climbed into the car and crouched as low as we could on the floor. We weren't yet out of the detention center's jurisdiction and feared they'd find us and take us back. It was just my dad, Debbie, and me riding together for what seemed like an eternity before we finally met up with my mom. I was so happy I'd escaped, and to be reunited with my parents. Speeding toward North Carolina, we stayed in two separate cars and switched passengers every now and again. Officially on the run, we had to keep moving to avoid arrest.

Still extremely upset that my friend, Debbie, was with us, what my mother did next was almost unforgivable.

Chapter 4

Journey Out West

"Not even the brightest future can make up for the fact
that no roads lead back to what came before —
to the innocence of childhood."
— Joe Nesbo

On the run and trying to figure out our next move, we stopped for fuel at a gas station in North Carolina. Debbie and I headed for the restroom and to grab some snacks. I made my way back to the car before Debbie and sat waiting with my mom. It was then that my mother, with no warning or discussion, decided to leave the gas station without Debbie. She was twelve years old … had no money, no phone (this was long before cell phones), no change of clothes. Just alone and abandoned on the side of an unfamiliar highway. My protests and shrieks of disbelief fell on deaf ears as my mother sped away from the gas station without a trace of emotion, heading toward Port Huron, Michigan.

To this day, I've never seen or heard from Debbie and I often wonder what happened to her. What did she do and how did she react when she realized we'd left without her? Did she make it back to the detention center alive? Did she go on to find happiness in her life? Or did she endure struggles far worse than mine? My heart hurts for her and I often dream of meeting up with her once more. I don't even remember crying that day. It all happened so fast that the memory is a blur to me today. Perhaps I blocked much of it out.

~

I feared meeting them again because I didn't know what my family might have done to them during our short stay in their home decades earlier. Did we steal from them? Lie to them?

~

My dad arranged for us to stay in Port Huron with his cousin, Bill, and his family, whom I'd never met. As we pulled up to their home and exited the Chevy Impala I'd wrecked a few months earlier, I noticed all the houses looked alike. It was a beautiful fall day and my cousins, along with a small army of other neighborhood kids, were outside riding bikes, throwing baseballs, and playing basketball. Not a lifestyle I was used to, and one I was able to enjoy only for a few days—the time it took Bill to learn the police were looking for us. So, we blew out of Port Huron almost as quickly as we'd blown in, lucky to leave before the authorities caught up with us.

Years later, when those same cousins found me on Facebook, they invited me and my kids to meet them in Detroit for a concert in which my cousin's son was playing. Truthfully, I feared meeting them again because I didn't know what my family might have done to them during our short stay in their home decades earlier. Did we steal from them? Lie to them? Would they remember and confront me or embarrass me? I decided to meet with them anyway, hoping they'd see I wasn't that same troubled kid. The reunion with my cousin, Ann, was unexpectedly powerful. She shared her memories of that first visit, describing my family as "a circus that came into town and that everyone wanted out of there immediately." Ann recalled me speaking of many things that, at the age of 12, struck her as odd, such as parties, drinking, sex, and all kinds of crazy activities that, at the time, constituted my normal. I have no recollection of many of the anecdotes she recounted, but anything is possible when you grow up as fast as I did.

After leaving Michigan, we traveled through the Dakotas, stopping at Mount Rushmore. I walked up to the area where there was no fencing, in awe of the massive monument. That is, until I noticed something slithering in the brush near my feet. It was my first encounter with a rattlesnake and I was back in the car in record time, ready to view South Dakota from the rear-view mirror.

We spent the next month or so on the road, heading toward the Pacific Northwest. I'm not sure how we paid for our hotel and food. Perhaps it was with the stolen credit cards that got my dad arrested, though he wasn't away long before he got out on bail and was reunited with us once more. Our next stop was Renton, Washington, where it rained nearly the entire time we were there, which was about a month. When the sun finally came out, I remember it hurting my eyes.

We stayed with my Aunt Shirley and her kids—my cousin David, who was eight years older than me, and my cousin Steven, who was my age. We were a bad influence on them, often smoking pot and getting high while Aunt Shirley and my dad argued over bills. Shortly after their final blow-up, we packed up and headed for California to meet up with my half-sister, Gena.

For as long as I could remember, Gena had lived with my grandmother. That is, until she ran away when she was around 16 years old. My mother hadn't seen her for over five years. Somehow, Mom re-established contact and arranged for us to live with Gena. As The Beach Boys filled our car with their musical wish that "they all could be California girls," I was about to become just that.

Chapter 5

Wild, Wild West

"I will scatter you among the nations and will draw out my sword and pursue you. Your land will be laid waste, and your cities will lie in ruins."
Leviticus 26:33 (NIV)

Life was like running with Ma Barker through the Wild West from the time we left our family in Michigan until we arrived in California in 1972. Along the way, we traveled through Canada, Ohio, North Dakota, and many other states, spending the nights in hotels, probably charged to someone else's credit cards. While I don't know how we afforded our lodging or food, I do know we ate. Later in life, I was always afraid to re-visit these places and families for fear of confronting the destruction we'd left behind.

California was the one stop I was truly looking forward to—sunny skies, beaches, becoming a California girl, and Hollywood stars! I was also excited to see Gena, who was nine years older than me.

It was daytime when we arrived in Southgate, seven miles southeast of downtown Los Angeles. I was thrilled to be in

California with Gena in her one-bedroom apartment. At 21, she was tall, blonde, tan, and pretty. I hadn't seen her since I was six and we didn't have a close relationship since we hadn't grown up together, but I was excited to get to know her. Gena lived with her boyfriend, Dan, who wasn't crazy about us staying with them.

~

Dan had shot a harpoon through the television. Obviously, we'd worn out our welcome.

~

I was adventurous, fearless, and loved to drive my mom's gold Plymouth everywhere, exploring my new surroundings. I distinctly remember walking to a phone booth to call my best friend, Reggie. Although I had to say good-bye to him when I left Virginia, we'd kept in touch. After ending the call, a stranger pulled up in his car, introduced himself as Tiny, and asked me if I wanted to be the secretary for Three Dog Night, a wildly popular LA-based band. Like a fool, I jumped into his car, thinking only of how awesome it would be to work for one of the country's hottest music groups. I took Tiny back to my sister's apartment, totally oblivious that he was actually trying to solicit me for sex. Turns out, Tiny was indeed a bus driver for famous musicians and he ended up enlisting my dad and brother to work with him. Over the years, they worked with Leon Russell, Billy Preston, and Led Zeppelin, even driving us around the beach one time in Elvis Presley's tricked-out tour bus. It didn't take me long to meet new people...after all, it was California in the freewheeling 1970s.

We didn't stay with my sister for long. Since Gena and Dan argued frequently, there was a lot of tension and little privacy in their small apartment. One day, while I was out exploring California, they got into a big fight. Upon returning to the apartment, I witnessed the resulting destruction: Dan had shot a harpoon through the television. Obviously, we'd worn out our welcome.

We moved into a motel for a few days and then into a Southgate apartment. After less than four months, we moved again, this time, into a rental in Bellflower, about an hour southeast of LA. Finally, for the first time since leaving Virginia, we had our own home!

It was late 1974 and the city was alive with music, hippies, cool cars cruising the boulevard, drugs, and crime. My brother became friends with hardened criminals through his job at a local decal company and started bringing home members of a group called Lynwood White Boys. These guys were party animals.

~

Enraged, we moved into instant retaliation mode
and unanimously decided to firebomb the gang's house.

~

At age 14, I hooked up with a 19-year-old named Richard. We would party all night and sleep all day, get up the next day, and do it all over again. We started off smoking pot, then moved to heavy drugs like cocaine, LSD, Quaaludes, Tuinal, and PCP in all its forms. Any drug you can think of, we were doing and it was going on all the time. I felt like I loved Richard, but, really, what did I know about love? We were in a relationship for about a year. All we did was get high and have sex. We went to the beach once and to the desert. But it was always about scoring the next drug and chasing the next high. Before long, the police knew me by my first name—not a good thing. People were coming and going from the house at all hours. No one worked except my brother, and we all sold drugs.

Our next move was into my brother's girlfriend's house in Lynwood. This house and this city are where everything spiraled out of control as we continued the party scene at an accelerated pace. Foot traffic—from gangsters to dope addicts—filed in and out of the house with increasing regularity. We had no discernment about anyone who wanted to come in and buy or sell drugs, or get wasted with us.

One night, a group of us left our house to party at a mutual friend's place. While there, we learned that a bike had been stolen earlier that day from our mutual friend's little brother. We suspected a notorious local gang was to blame. Wielding pipes, chains, and baseball bats, our group left the party to retrieve the bike, find the gang members, and give them a beating they'd never forget. Sure enough, we found the suspects, exchanged hostile words, and the fight was on. After inflicting a bloody beat-down, we returned to the party.

Everyone was inside except for a guy named Larry and a few others, who were hanging out in the front yard. Suddenly, from inside, we heard loud screaming and someone shouting, "They're here!" Chaos erupted as we ran into each other in the narrow hallway, frantically scrambling to exit the house. Meanwhile, the gang members had busted Larry's skull open with a tire iron and he was rushed by ambulance to the hospital.

Enraged, we moved into instant retaliation mode and unanimously decided to firebomb the gang's house. As our mob set off to take care of business, my thoughts raced and my nerves seemed unhinged. We'd originally planned to siphon fuel out of cars and fill two wine bottles with the gasoline. Instead, we purchased gasoline, filled the bottles, and stuffed a sock into the neck of each one. Loaded up in two cars—each carrying one firebomb—the tension was palpable as we approached our target, hoping we could throw our Molotov cocktails into the house and flee the scene before the gang members had time to retaliate. But even if they confronted us, we were prepared for anything. We had chains if we had to fight again, and we had our firebombs ready to deploy.

Seconds after the two firebombs crashed into the home's front window, we could see flames spreading everywhere. We peeled off, only to be pulled over by a pair of Lynwood police officers who urged us to flee the scene immediately for our own safety. Realizing that we were responsible for the attack, the gang firebombed our party house, but we were long gone. Unfortunately, the home's permanent residents were inside when the house was set ablaze, though they managed to escape uninjured. Later that week, the Lynwood Police Department made arrests and I was among those apprehended.

Though I was 14 years old, my fake ID said I was 18. So, rather than being treated as a juvenile, I was taken to the Los Angeles County Jail. Totally terrified, I entered kicking and screaming. They forced me into a cold, grey room to strip-search me but, before they could remove my clothes, I cried out, "You can't do this to me! I'm only a child! I'm fourteen!" I gave them my date of birth and birthplace and continued yelling about being a minor. The officer charged with searching me stopped and listened. The Correction Officers processing inmates told the arresting officer he couldn't receive me because of my age, so the officer escorted me back to his car and told me he was taking me to juvenile hall. I immediately felt relief.

Once we arrived at the juvenile hall, however, they wouldn't receive me, either. My ID said I was 18. They told the officer he would have to straighten this out before anyone could take me. I was driven back to the Lynwood Police Department, where I was released. With no one to pick me up, I walked home, knowing that everyone else involved in the firebombing had been arrested. I can't remember who was at home when I got there. My mom and brother were in jail. My dad was on the road. Feeling relieved, like I'd pulled off an unbelievable feat, I was ready to get back to the party life I'd been living. This was one of the many times I found myself in handcuffs while somehow escaping a long-term sentence.

Chapter 6

My Shutdown

"Of all the things trauma takes away from us,
the worst is our willingness, or even our ability, to be vulnerable.
There's a reclaiming that has to happen."
— Brené Brown

My relationship with Richard ended abruptly when he broke up with me. Though he was a mess, everyone blamed me for the split. His mother wanted him to get his life back on track and said that would never happen if we were still together. I didn't see the break-up coming, and when it happened it felt like my whole world was caving in. Though my young heart was shattered, it was instantly revitalized when I met … Frank.

Frank was five years older than me and the lifelong friend of a foster child named Chuck, who'd moved into our house in Lynnwood. A high school senior, Frank was well-mannered, driven, and exciting. Unlike the other guys I'd been with, Frank seemed to have it together, including plans for a great future. He was also incredibly handsome—with long, Fabio-like hair blowing in the Southern California breeze. I was highly attracted to this older, intriguing stranger who seemed to ride into my life on a proverbial white stallion. We both felt like a magnet had instantly drawn our hearts together.

Frank had no idea how old I was and, when he found out, he was furious. Had anyone exposed to the authorities our sexual activity, my minor status alone could have destroyed Frank's plans for his future. But our secret was safe. And, with only months until graduation from Lynwood High, Frank started coming around more often. Gradually, as he realized he could party with me more and attend school less, he eventually dropped out. Our days and nights were filled with 24/7 parties. The more we used drugs, the more people came; and the more people who came, the more drugs we sold, earning money to supply our demand. Frank quickly escalated into heavier drug use and ultimately ended up addicted to PCP, an upper that causes hallucinations and excitement.

In the craziness of the drugs and sex, a physical fight broke out between Frank, Richard, and Chuck. At the time, I didn't understand why they'd fought; later, I was told that it might have had something to do with me. During the fight, Frank was stabbed in the groin and lost so much blood that doctors feared he might not survive.

Richard was arrested for the stabbing but eventually was released because of a lack of evidence. Frank had surgery and, after a lengthy recovery, was released to go home. Chuck fled the scene before the police and ambulance arrived, leaving his best friend, Frank, to fend for himself. When Frank came home from the hospital, he stayed with me, and I helped care for and monitor him. We were inseparable after that. Frank moved in with me and my family in the house in Lynwood. This was the best-case scenario for me to fast-track our future together. My vision had always been to find a dream man, move out of my parents' house, establish my own life, and, finally, escape the chaos of our broken family.

Convinced that I was living with the man of my dreams, I decided to start applying for a job. I was hired as a Taco Bell shift worker, picking up swing shifts from 3 p.m. to 11 p.m. I worked hard and gradually moved up to Shift Supervisor.

~

I grabbed the welcome mat at their doorstep
to cover myself—bloody, humiliated, and vulnerable.

~

I owned a Plymouth Fury III, a wrecked junker with a wooden bumper, drooping headliner, and push-button gears. It was a reliable mess that got me from point A to point B. One night, I left Frank with the car and went to work. Frank was supposed to pick me up that evening after I finished my shift. With no cell phones, no internet, and no way to track someone down, I called repeatedly from my work phone but was unable to connect with Frank. Knowing that he was sitting at home getting high, I set off for our house on foot, angry and disappointed. The walk was long and I was power-walking while stewing over what I'd say to Frank when I arrived. Fearless and totally preoccupied in anger, I never even considered my safety or surroundings as I stepped off the curb on Imperial Highway that night.

The moment my foot hit the ground beneath the curb, I was grabbed from behind. Another assailant jumped in front of me and, together, they threw me into the back seat of a car, where I saw two more guys in the front seat. They cruised the dark streets of various LA suburbs while taking turns sexually assaulting me. It was the most terrifying ride of my life. Scared and confused, my mind quickly pivoted from anger to survival. After what seemed like hours, they slowed down and threw me out of the car, naked. I jumped up and ran as quickly as I could to the first house I saw. I grabbed the welcome mat at their doorstep to cover myself—bloody, humiliated, and vulnerable. Then I pounded on the door and screamed until a bleary-eyed couple opened it. Their horror quickly turned to compassion as they called the police and grabbed a robe for me to put on. Frank, however, was still MIA.

Sitting in shock, I was unable to process anything as the police arrived. They knew me and were not surprised to see me. In fact, they didn't take me seriously and even jokingly speculated about what I'd done to cause the rape. I can't remember the details of what transpired after I talked to the police. I don't know if a rape kit was used to collect evidence, how I was taken to the hospital, or how I got home from the hospital. Silently, I moved from survival mode to completely shutting down, passively letting others handle the details of my case. The shutdown lasted 17 more years as my recreational drug use spiraled into non-stop self-medication and drug abuse to numb my mind from this unspeakably painful experience.

When I got home the next day, Frank was still passed out from his night of partying. As he came to, it was clear he'd never even noticed my absence the night before. Nor did he notice my physical appearance. I was no longer filled with the rage that had consumed me before the rape. I was too numb even to care anymore. I gave Frank the CliffsNotes version of the crime perpetrated against me and expected him to apologize for abandoning his responsibilities to pick me up from work. Instead, he announced that I was the only one responsible. We never spoke of the incident again.

It was late 1975, and I began to self-medicate with downers so I could spend more time trying to sleep away my depression. A part of me was dead for the next 17 years, though I still worked at Taco Bell and continued to live with Frank. I was in denial and steadfastly committed to a doomed relationship.

Chapter 7

Addicted to Betrayal

"So much of what we learn about love is taught
by people who never really loved us."
— Unknown

The first part of 1976 was marked by good times, traveling for two and three weeks at a time in my dad's 18-wheeler with my mom and Vicki, a friend with whom I continued the party scene while on the road. My dad was a truck driver and this was the perfect opportunity for me to enjoy a little time away from Frank—who was living in my parents' Lynwood house—though I periodically checked in with him. We had a great time as we wheeled our way toward Ohio to pick up a child as a result of my mother's decision to resume fostering. The youngster would be one of the many kids who came to live in our home over the next several years.

A few months after returning from Ohio, I flew to Boston for a family funeral and, upon my return, my brother, Steven, told me that he and Frank had met some girls at a fast-food restaurant while I was in Boston. They brought them back home and Frank had cheated on me with one of them. I was devastated. I confronted Frank, but he assured me it was a meaningless fling and that he would never do it again. I loved him and believed he was telling the truth. Even so, we began to argue and fight more.

~

**I grabbed my mother's gun and set out to confront Frank.
"If he won't tell me the truth, maybe a little fear
will motivate him...."**

~

Eventually, he moved back home with his parents. Although we could barely get along, I wasn't sure if my heart could stand the desperate ache I felt when we were apart. Frank was the most important person in my life and I wanted him back home with me. With him gone, I spent more time in my head blaming myself for not trusting him. At some point during our separation, my parents moved from Lynwood back to Bellflower.

Not long after Frank moved out, my brother told me that Frank had cheated on me again. As my rage grew, I had to know the truth. I grabbed my mother's gun and set out to confront Frank. *If he won't tell me the truth, maybe a little fear will motivate him,* I thought as I drove to his parents' house. Frank was asleep when I arrived, so his parents woke him up. When he came to the door, he suggested we step outside. We walked to the garage, where I asked him point-blank, "Did you cheat on me?"

He didn't even answer; he just slapped me across the face and asked, "Now do you believe me?" I responded, "No, I don't." Before I could finish my sentence, he punched me in the face with a closed fist, knocking me off my chair onto the ground. I saw my purse out of the corner of my eye and instantly remembered the gun. I grabbed my purse, pulled out the gun, and pointed it at him. "You need to tell me the truth," I demanded. "Did you cheat on me?"

Frank bolted inside his house, yelling back at me, "I'm calling the police! What are you, crazy?" Afraid, enraged, and unsure of my next move, I ran back to my car. Then, still wielding the gun, I ran toward a friend's house, two doors down. Before I could go inside, the police arrived from both directions. I took out the bullets and dropped them on the ground. Guns drawn and ready to fire, they had me surrounded. I lowered my pistol and they arrested me as Frank looked on, yelling, "Get her out of here, she's crazy!" I wasn't crazy, just broken-hearted.

The police took me to the Sybil Brand Institute in LA Country. I called Frank from the jail and he took my call. I asked him again if he'd cheated on me. He stuck to his story and said no. I asked him to swear on his dad's life but he refused. Finally, Frank remorsefully confessed and said he didn't mean to hurt me. He promised he would never again be unfaithful, adding that me pulling a gun on him was far worse than anything he'd ever done. I was broken, and that's enough to make a sane person crazy.

~

**It didn't matter how often Frank hurt me,
I was desperate to be with him.**

~

My charges were reduced from attempted murder to brandishing a loaded gun in public. I don't remember who bailed me out that day, but I remember waking up in Frank's arms. He had stayed with me at my parents' house that night. What a wonderful feeling waking up with him. Yet, I sensed weird vibes. Was he holding a grudge? Deep down, did he really forgive me for pulling the gun on him? I decided I could live with the ambivalence. *I forgave him, so he must have genuinely forgiven me,* I told myself.

Looking back, I now see that this incident was a turning point for me. I loved Frank more than life itself and began praying regularly for God to help our relationship. I started attending church on Sundays for the first time since I lived in Virginia. I hoped that, if I reconnected with God, my heart would stop hurting.

The day after I was released from jail, Frank went home and I went to a friend's house. We sat around, drank a few beers, and I stayed for dinner. It was a good time. When I went home, Frank was at my house, furious because I wasn't there when he arrived. After some angry words, he walked away, but I jumped in my car and caught up with him. As I sat in my car, talking to him with the window rolled down, he punched me in the head. Instead of leaving, we continued arguing, then, finally, we returned home to smoke a joint and continue our argument.

After little while, Frank left again but, first, hid my car keys. I ran after him, calling to him, but he wouldn't stop. I turned and returned home, found my car keys, and drove to Frank's house, arriving before he did. When he saw me at his house, he hit me in the face, busting my lip open. Then, he grabbed me and dragged me to his parents' backyard while saying he should kill me. Blood covered my hands and face. Finally, as though a switch had flipped off, Frank took me into the garage and cleaned me up, treating me with tenderness. Shaken and hurt, both physically and emotionally, I told Frank to call me when he could treat me like a lady. In truth, though, he and I both understood: It didn't matter how often Frank hurt me, I was desperate to be with him.

When I saw Frank again a few days later, I told him I wanted to get married, have his baby, and care for him the rest of his life. I believed that, if we were meant to be together, he would come back. A week after the last beating, Frank showed up at my parents' house. He seemed really happy and said he had a surprise for me. I ran to him and hugged him as he proudly presented me with two Angel Dust joints. We went into the closet and smoked, then he went outside and found two pieces of telephone wire that he fashioned into an engagement ring. We made love, and life seemed so special, so perfect. I treasured every moment, thrilled to have him in my arms again and eager to spend the rest of my life with him.

We had several more arguments that resulted in our separation throughout the rest of 1976. But, each time, I blamed myself for screwing up our relationship. I cried desperately in pain to have him come back, swearing I wouldn't mess up again. In constant self-blame and denial about the abuse and co-dependency, I continued to pursue Frank no matter the cost.

Chapter 8

The Birth of a Mother

"What we are suffering now cannot compare
with the glory that will be shown to us."
— Romans 8:18 (CEV)

Though our relationship was sometimes on and sometimes off, Frank and I were getting along well around the time I realized I'd missed my period and had an idea that I may be pregnant. I went in for a pregnancy test at the Pregnancy Clinic in Downey, California. Later that day, after my check-up, I met up with Frank. He wanted to know what the doctors had said. "We're going to have a baby," I told him.

Our baby was due in November of 1977 and, while Frank and my mother were both excited, I was nervous. Frank initially tried to stay involved. I believed being pregnant would fix our relationship and we would finally be a happy family. I felt torn; I'd always wondered if I would be a good mother and if Frank would really love me and the baby like I wanted him to. I began cleaning up my lifestyle in response to parenthood, but not Frank. He continued partying and spending time with friends instead of focusing on us and our future. His irresponsibility was deeply hurtful. While Frank was out enjoying life, I was crying my eyes out at home. I desperately desired to have a good man in my life, yet Frank's and my relationship was continually on edge.

As expectant parents, Frank and I decided it was time to get our own place, so we moved from my parents' house in Bellflower into an apartment in Long Beach. We started accumulating things for the baby and I was getting excited about our new arrival. I was gaining weight and my body was quickly changing. Knowing I was going to have a baby was such a wonderful feeling. I quit drinking, smoking, and doing drugs, and was healthier than I'd ever been. Frank seemed happier, too, and even went job hunting. Though we still were struggling in our relationship, Frank said he wanted to get married before the baby came, and we enjoyed spending time talking about baby-name options for both boys and girls.

During this time, my best friend, Vicki, had a baby. Seeing her little one made me even more excited about mine. Frank, however, wasn't emotionally available or physically present though I yearned for his companionship. It felt like the more I tried to work things out, the more we were pulled apart. I desperately wanted us to figure this out before the baby came. Instead, we argued all the time.

Frank finally got a job at Lynwood's St. Francis Hospital in September, two months before our baby's due date. He really enjoyed his job, which seemed to help him stay focused on us and our future. We continued attending our childbirth classes and were getting along better. Our friends and family were completely supportive of us. My mom threw us a beautiful baby shower and things seemed to be going amazingly well … until Frank disappeared one night. After a few days, he showed up at our house to pick up his gun and some other belongings, clearly intending to leave again.

~

Frank was sitting in a chair facing the front door. Propped up next to him was his Winchester 3030 rifle and he was holding his baseball bat.

~

When he arrived, we got into a heated argument about where he'd been. Shortly after that, Frank slapped me in the face and then destroyed our apartment with a baseball bat. As he was breaking apart our bedroom dresser, in tears of desperation, I ran to my neighbors' and called the police. This marked the first time in our relationship I'd ever called the authorities. Frank had no idea I'd placed the call, but I was outside waiting for the police when they showed up. As I escorted them inside, Frank was sitting in a chair facing the front door. Propped up next to him was his Winchester 3030 rifle and he was holding his baseball bat. I locked eyes with him when I walked in. The look on his face told me he was barely getting started.

When I saw his gun, I immediately stepped aside and allowed the police to take over. The officer talked Frank into moving away from the gun and, gradually, Frank's demeanor changed as the situation was skillfully de-escalated. The police confiscated Frank's gun and made him leave our apartment. A few days later, I received a handwritten note from Frank telling me how sorry he was. I believed him and eventually invited him to come back home. Considering the episode "water under the bridge," we never discussed it again, though I continued walking on eggshells around him.

I was feeling anxious about having the baby but I couldn't communicate with Frank about what I was going through. He had no sympathy for me or my anxiety. Instead, he called me names like "fat whale." His goal was to ensure I would focus on losing weight after the baby was born.

Near the end of my pregnancy, tired of wearing maternity clothes and ready to hold my baby, I woke up with sharp pains the morning of November 15, 1977, thinking it was time. I sat in the bathroom reading a book on how to know if you're in labor. Anxious, I didn't want to wake up Frank for a false alarm. He'd warned me before not to keep him up or at the hospital for too long. I didn't know what to expect; I just knew I didn't want to inconvenience him.

After a few hours of pressure, I woke Frank. Feeling like I had to go to the bathroom, I knew it was time. Frank asked me if I was sure I was in labor and I said yes. On the drive to the hospital, I said I had to use the bathroom. Frank pulled over and I tried to go, but I couldn't. The baby was coming. At the hospital, they checked me in and brought me a wheelchair, but I couldn't even sit. The nurse told me to relax and said my labor could easily last about 14 hours. They took me to my room and, again, I went to use the bathroom. I was in there for a few minutes when the nurse came to check on me. I told her I couldn't go to the bathroom, though I felt an urgent need. The nurse checked me, felt the baby's head crowning, and rushed me to the delivery room. Less than an hour later, at 6:55 a.m., our adorable 8-pound 2.5-ounce baby was born.

A nurse placed the warm, wet bundle on my chest and announced it was a girl. We named her Lisa Marie. I was in shock and awe, overwhelmed with emotion. The instant I saw her, I fell deeply in love. In that brief moment, her whole future flashed before my eyes and I made a solemn promise that Lisa would never live the life I had lived. I knew she was an undeserved gift and I felt privileged to have this beautiful life in my hands. From that moment on, I was responsible for Lisa and determined to give her the best life possible.

It wasn't about me anymore. It was all about her. A daughter and a mother were both born that day.

We stayed at the hospital for a couple of days. (Back then, they kept you a little longer to ensure everyone was healthy before sending you home.) Frank seemed very happy about Lisa's arrival. She was beautiful and slept a lot and we loved her more than words could express. Frank worked hard every day to support us, and I continued to bond with Lisa over the next several months. We shopped together, spent our first Christmas together, and I absolutely loved my new role as a mother. Frank and I were getting along better, as well. Finally, our lives were settling down and we were one happy family. Or so I thought.

.

Chapter 9

No Coming Back

"Bye-bye, baby, it's been a sweet love, though this feeling I can't change,
but please don't take it so badly, cause Lord knows I'm to blame.
But, if I stayed here with you, girl, things just couldn't be the same,
'cause I'm as free as a bird now, and this bird you'll never change."
— Lynyrd Skynyrd, "Free Bird"

After Christmas of 1977, Frank and I were invited to move into the manager's house in front of our apartments, rent-free, in exchange for helping to collect rent from the other tenants. Frank continued to work while I stayed home and cared for Lisa, who'd grown colicky and was unable to sleep. I wasn't getting much sleep, either—a reality of motherhood that, at times, made me cry right along with my baby. It was hard to keep Frank happy with a crying baby. He complained that he had to be up for work early and I needed to "shut that baby up." He spent more time working, and I felt like he really wanted to make a good life for us. While he didn't party as much as he had before Lisa's birth, his escalating drug use led our family into a downward spiral.

In February of the following year, Frank started planning a birthday party for my mother. The two had been close since Frank and I started dating. Mostly, they bonded over their shared love for drugs and partying. Mom was a chameleon, morphing into whoever you wanted or needed her to be at any given moment. Frank wanted to host the party at our house but, between working and caring for our baby, I opposed the plan. (Later, I learned that Frank had announced the party's location even before mentioning the idea to me.)

~

"It doesn't matter what religion you are.
What matters is that you stay close to God."

~

On the day of the big event, throngs of people poured into our already-cramped house. That night, I was expecting everyone to leave. Instead, Frank invited them all to stay. Lisa and I sequestered ourselves in the bedroom as what was meant to be a birthday party turned into a three-day drug- and party-fest. I was disgusted and irritated with Frank and my mother. This was not the safe, wholesome lifestyle I'd envisioned for our daughter. I wanted to escape but had nowhere to go. I felt completely stuck. Meanwhile, Frank and I continued to argue and fight. He wasn't changing, and I knew I wanted better for my life and our daughter.

A few days later, my mother called, alarmed, saying that my brother, Steven, was high. She asked us to come over ASAP and intervene. Frank didn't want to go, but said Mom had done so much for us and that we needed to be there for her. So we grabbed Lisa and headed to my mother's house in Bellflower. When we arrived, Steven wasn't there and my mother was loaded. Later, after Steven returned, mother asked Frank to take my brother home and pick up some Angel Dust on his way back. When he left, I asked him not to

58

be out too late; I was tired and ready to go home. Frank kissed me good-bye and said he'd be back before long. I fell asleep in my old bed with Lisa in the crib.

At 2 a.m., Frank woke me from a deep sleep and immediately started telling me that I looked like a hussy. Irritated, I said I didn't know what he was talking about. Then, Lisa started to wake up and I got upset. I told Frank to go home and get some rest since he had to be up in a few short hours for work. He began yelling and took off in my mother's car. My mom called him 20 minutes later and Frank told her to come pick up her car at our home in Long Beach; he was going to sleep. Leaving Lisa in the care of a friend, we left right away and, upon arriving at my house, I noticed Frank sitting in my mother's car. Immediately upon seeing us, he careened out of the driveway and took off. A high-speed chase ensued, nearing 100 miles per hour at times. We ran red lights and sped down one-way streets. Finally, the police stopped me. I yelled at them, "Get the purple Gremlin! He's going to kill himself!"

The police took off after Frank and I pursued the police, but couldn't keep up. So I dropped my mom off at her house in Bellflower and continued my pursuit of the police and Frank. After a while, I gave up and dropped by my brother's house. I asked them what Frank was high on, since he was out of his mind. Their reply: vodka and Angel Dust. It was 4:30 a.m. by the time I tracked down Frank's drug dealer. I asked her if Frank had been there earlier and, if so, what was he loaded on. She said she didn't know what I was talking about. I left there crying and scared, aware that the police probably were still chasing Frank.

Frank had always insisted that I not tell his parents about his drug use, but now I felt compelled to break my silence. Arriving at their home, I woke his mom and dad up and filled them in. Of course, they were shocked and alarmed. I left there and went to my mother's house, asking Frank's parents to call if they heard anything. Mother was on the phone with the police when I arrived. I could tell they knew something but wouldn't tell her. Screaming and crying, I grabbed the phone and begged them to tell me what was going on.

"Where is he?" I pleaded. "Is he alright? In jail? Is he OK?"

"No, he's not," came the reply, followed by interminable silence.

"Is he at the hospital? Is he hurt? Where is he?" I screamed. Then came the answer I'd been dreading: "Ma'am, he is dead."

It felt like a load of bricks had fallen on me full force, knocking me to the floor. When I was finally able to talk, I asked more questions and the officer volunteered to send a detective over to fill me in. One thing needed no clarification: three-month-old Lisa's father was dead and my whole future collapsed.

Frank and I had tried so many times before to make things better but, this time, I was powerless to fix our shattered reality. After driving to his parents' house to break the news, I headed to my mom's, crying inconsolably. I could talk to no one and I felt like I couldn't trust anyone, either. I was completely confused and desperate to know what had happened to Frank after he left my mother's house the night before.

Later that day, a detective arrived at my mother's house and recounted the events leading to Frank's death. The police report indicated Frank was out of control, waving and shooting his gun out of his car's driver's side window as police pursued him at high speed for 24 miles. Eventually, police blew out the hatchback's window with gunfire and Frank pulled over, got out of the car, and dropped his gun. But as police tried to handcuff and arrest him, Frank resisted and lunged for an officer's gun. A fellow policeman reacted instantly, fatally shooting Frank in the forehead. He was pronounced dead on arrival at the hospital. Also DOA that night: my dreams of having a happy, healthy family.

A few days before Frank's funeral, I went to St. Francis Hospital, where Frank had worked, to pick up a donation the staff had collected to help with funeral expenses. Upon arriving, I met a kind nun who handed me the collection envelope. After extending her condolences and chatting for a few minutes, to my surprise, she asked, "Debbie, what religion are you?" I had no earthly idea what to say. *Here goes*, I thought. *Since she's Catholic, she's going to try to convert me.* Sitting in silence, I didn't answer the question.

The nun talked about other things for a few more minutes, then excused herself and went to her office. She returned with a Good News version of the Bible, which she presented to me as a gift. I thanked her, said good-bye, and headed for the door. Then, I heard my name, so I paused and turned back. "Debbie," she called to me, "It doesn't matter what religion you are. What matters is that you stay close to God." Her words penetrated deep into my soul. It was another "God moment" like the one I'd experienced years before with Brother Caewood. My Heavenly Father again used one of His servants—this time, a Catholic sister—to share His truth and teach me about prioritizing my relationship with Jesus.

On the day of Frank's funeral, I was emotionally numb. Everything seemed surreal. Frank's family had made all of the funeral arrangements without so much as consulting me. Since we'd never married, my wishes—my voice—didn't seem to matter. I had not only lost my baby's father but, now, I was being treated as if I'd never existed in Frank's life.

Frank's family wanted his body moved from the Los Angeles Coroner's office to Rose Hills Memorial Park in Whittier. Deeply hurt and angered, I decided, *If they're going to treat me as if I'm invisible,*

I'm not going to sign the transfer papers. After a brief standoff, a family member called and urged me to cooperate—which I did, grudgingly. I fumed on my drive to the Memorial Park, unable to understand how they could treat me as though I'd meant nothing to Frank.

~

He taught me that the love I had been searching for in Frank would never come to me in the form of a person.

~

By the time I arrived, however, Frank's family's icy attitude had melted, which helped calm my own frazzled nerves. They were all genuinely nice to me. Looking back, I realize I wasn't in any position, emotionally or financially, to handle the stress of making funeral arrangements. I also recognize that, like me, Frank's family was grief-stricken and simply trying to bury their son as quickly as possible so they could put this excruciating ordeal behind them.

I thought the day of Frank's funeral would be the last time I would see or speak to him. I had no idea I would continue to see him repeatedly in my mind, which I feared I was losing. I visited Frank's gravesite every day and even talked to his pictures on the wall. It was about six months before I could breathe again.

Journaling in my diary was comforting, as was drawing closer to God, which I began doing about three months after Frank's funeral. During this period, I dedicated Lisa to the Lord and God began to give me peace, though at the time I didn't realize it. My life's trajectory had been set on a brand-new path. God was pursuing me and slowly taking away my pain. He showed me that I needed to keep my eyes on Him if I wanted to be healed. I prayed for the Lord to be my teacher. I wanted Him to teach me the things I needed to know about the Bible and to re-build the faith I'd had as a child. The Lord began revealing truths, and He didn't stop. He taught me that the love I had been searching for in Frank would never come to me in the form of a person. God showed me through this song that He was the Love I'd always wanted and needed:

You said You'd come

And share all my sorrows

You said You'd be there

For all my tomorrows

I came so close to sending You away

But just like You promised

You came there to stay

I just had to pray

Chorus

And Jesus said

Come to the water

Stand by My side

I know you are thirsty

You won't be denied

I felt every teardrop

When in darkness you cried

And I strove to remind you

That for those tears I died

Your goodness so great

I can't understand

And dear Lord I know

That all this was planned

I know You're here now

And always will be
Your love loosed my chains
And in You, I'm free
But Jesus, why me?

Jesus, I give You
My heart and my soul
I know that without God
I'd never be whole
Savior, You opened
All the right doors
And I thank You and praise You
From earth's humble shores
Take me, I'm Yours"[2]

---

[2] Marsha Stevens, "For Those Tears I Died."

Part Two

Chapter 10

Disobedience Brings Consequences

"Don't be misled; remember that you can't ignore God and get away with it: a man will always reap just the kind of crop he sows!"
– Galatians 6:7 (TLB)

After Frank's funeral, I returned to our Long Beach home to find that it had been burglarized. Back in those days, home addresses, funeral times, and other details were included in obituaries, making the unoccupied homes of grieving funeral-goers easy targets. A missing doorknob—completely removed by a vise grip—was my first clue that something was terribly wrong. My home was ransacked. Every drawer was pulled out, probably by someone looking for money. Everything they could possibly take was taken. Towels, bed sheets, coins, and all kinds of things that had no value to anyone but me. The police added to the mess with their fingerprinting process. Distraught and crying hysterically, I tried to restore some semblance of order as I silently asked, *Why is this happening to me?* I felt horribly violated yet again and I was afraid someone would come back to harm Lisa and me. I left the house that night and spent the next few weeks with Lisa living at my mother's house.

~

It felt like I'd walked into a crazy party; only, here, Jesus was the center of attention.

~

Feeling like my world was imploding and seeking comfort and stability, I started attending church for the first time since my childhood. Calvary Chapel in Downey had an intimate, family feel and only about 250 members. The pastor, Jeff Johnson, was young and relatable. He made the church a welcoming place, and I immediately plugged into every activity I could find. Through word-of-mouth publicity, these events always were packed and brimming with excitement. It felt like I'd walked into a crazy party; only, here, Jesus was the center of attention. The music was changing with the culture. It seemed like these free-spirited Christians were looking for a place to freely express their faith, and they found it at Calvary Chapel. People of all backgrounds—long-haired hippies, business people, women of all ages, children, and teens—were coming together to worship Jesus.

The church quickly outgrew its small home and began offering Sunday services at Downey Community Theatre. Hungry for connection, I signed up for anything and everything: After checking Lisa into the nursery, I taught Sunday School ... attended events almost every night of the week, including those for singles and single parents ... went to Wednesday-night services ... Friday movie night ... Saturday concerts ... and Sunday-morning church services.

As I filled my time with activities that nurtured my new-found love for Jesus, my life was changing and I began to distance myself from old friends. I tried to build friendships at Calvary Chapel, but those didn't last long. Ashamed, I never opened up to anyone about the dangerous lifestyle I'd led before joining the church. I didn't want anything to disrupt the joy and peace I found in the church and thought that hiding my past and maintaining a new, squeaky-clean image would simplify my life. I was trying to have a right relationship with God without authenticity.

A few weeks after Frank's death, we moved out of my mom's place and into a small, one-bedroom, one-bathroom apartment in Lynwood. One day, not long after, I answered the phone to hear a voice from my past. It was Tiny (the guy who solicited me to work for Three Dog Night), asking if I'd like a job in the security business. The job was to dispatch authorities when alarm signals came in, and dispatch technicians to maintain and service commercial and residential alarm systems. I immediately inquired about the job, and they set up an interview for the following day. I was excited about the opportunity but unsure of what to expect. During the interview, they mentioned needing to run a statewide background check on me. I was nervous, yet still made sure they knew I had to have Sundays off for church services. Miraculously, I was hired and started the job right away. This was my entrance into a 34-year career in the security industry.

At last, I felt like I could breathe, like there was hope for my future again. I had a stable job, was plugged into a loving church family, and my daughter and I had our own place. Though I wasn't even 18 years old, I had lived through so much chaos and destruction. Lisa and I had our whole future ahead of us, and I believed that if I kept my eyes on the Lord, we'd be okay.

My work environment was draining. Because we were

understaffed and the company operated 24/7, I spent many late nights and overnights at work. Everyone seemed content with their jobs, we all got along well, and my manager was super nice. As the dispatcher, I got to know and became close to everyone. We all carried on with fun jokes and created a light atmosphere.

~

I didn't want to smoke with Lloyd that night and I could have said no. But my intense desire for a stable relationship won the battle warring within.

~

When Lloyd, the service technician supervisor, started flirting with me, I wasn't immediately attracted to him, though I did appreciate the stability he could offer Lisa and me. As he pursued me, though, I became more interested. He was a gorgeous, dark-haired, Portuguese hottie with a nice build, dark mustache, and soulful brown eyes that made me melt. Lloyd and I began dating and, one night during dinner, he asked me to pick up a Sherman (a PCP cigarette) for a friend of his. In my heart, I didn't want to do it, but I wanted to avoid the possibility of losing Lloyd. When I brought it to his home, he lit it up and asked me to take a couple of hits with him.

I'd been clean for over three years and was scared that the old Debbie would come back. However, I saw Lloyd as offering the picture-perfect relationship—he had a job, he was stable, and he seemed to have it all together. I didn't want to smoke with Lloyd that night, and I could have said no. But my intense desire for a stable relationship won the battle warring within. I took a hit, and we became inseparable after that night—together whenever we weren't at work.

I wasn't used to going out on dates, so this was a new and exciting experience for me. As our relationship progressed even further, I became pregnant. I was hesitant to marry Lloyd, but I didn't want to have another child out of wedlock—especially because of my experience after Frank's death, when I found myself shut out of funeral planning because I wasn't, legally, his wife. Every decision in my life was motivated by my strong desire for stability. So, six months into my pregnancy with my daughter, Amy Joy, Lloyd and I married. With him, I thought, I would finally have the picture-perfect family I had longed for with Frank. I didn't realize that Lloyd, too, had a drug problem, which would turn our marriage into a nightmare.

Many nights, he wouldn't come home and I never knew where he was. One night, I was so tired of it all that I drove around until I found his van, which was parked in front of the house of one of the girls from our office. I knocked on the door. Nobody answered. Steaming mad, I entered the van, unlocked the parking brake, and watched the van roll downhill, ultimately smashing into a parked car. I shook my head as I walked away. Things never improved.

In 1985, my Dad passed away from a massive heart attack. Shortly afterward, I filed for divorce. Lloyd died of a drug overdose on December 4, 2002.

Chapter 11

I Wasn't Looking

"Sometimes, what you're looking for comes when you're not looking."
— Unknown

It was 1993 and Lisa was 15 years old, attending church regularly, and very involved in her youth group. Uncharacteristically, she kept bugging me to meet Kevin, the high school counselor who worked at our church. I wasn't really interested in meeting anyone, but Kevin caught my attention one day when I dropped by church and he rode by on a bicycle. Actually, his bike shorts grabbed my attention: they were cute and tight. He circled around me twice in the parking lot. Tall, with dark, long, curly hair, he struck me as strong and self-confident.

Kevin had two boys from two previous relationships, just as I had two girls from two fathers. It seemed hypocritical that I didn't want to date anyone with kids, but I didn't want to deal with all the problems that can accompany a blended family. Kevin was so good with his kids, Lisa adored him, and the two shared a close relationship. I also later learned that they were plotting behind my back to work him into my life. I would see Kevin randomly at church when picking up Lisa. At first, we got to know one another as friends and spent hours talking on the phone. Kevin pursued me through a courtship like I'd never experienced. Our first dates were so innocent and simple. He would put flowers on my pew at church, hold my hand, and treat me with great respect, something I'd never known. He sent me my first-ever love letter, which stole my heart. I was head-over-heels in love.

One evening, we rode in Kevin's mint-condition Volkswagen van to Belmont Shores Beach for a date. The fact that he'd planned ahead to create a special evening was endearing and exciting. It was a beautiful night, the stars were out, and the weather was perfect. There weren't many people around as we walked along the beach holding hands. At one point, he stopped and asked if it was okay to kiss me. I said yes, blown away that he'd asked my permission. He talked about marriage and how great it would be. I listened intently, but with serious reservations. I knew I wanted to be in a relationship, but I'd never known what a good marriage looked like. I told Kevin how I felt about marriage and he told me our marriage would be good. It didn't take long for our relationship to get serious after that night.

Shortly after our beach date, Kevin and Lisa went on a three-week youth trip called Mission America, a trip across America to share Jesus. As they traveled, Kevin kept in contact with me and wrote letters to update me about how Lisa was doing on the road. I could feel the chemistry brewing between us as his letters penetrated my heart. I not only saw his love for my daughter, but also a potential future with Kevin.

During this time, Security Signal Devices purchased Kern Security in Bakersfield. I commuted back and forth regularly to evaluate the newly acquired business and report back to my boss. When Lisa and Kevin returned from the mission trip, Kevin invited me to his parents' fortieth-anniversary party, introducing me to his family as the woman who was going to be his wife. Lacking the boldness I have now, I just smiled, unsure of what to say. Although it was surprising, it was still nice to hear him say it. Less than a month later, we purchased engagement and wedding rings and began six weeks of pre-marital counseling at our church.

As part of the counseling, we had to listen to pre-recorded messages and complete various assignments, including discussing the meaning of Ephesians 5:22 in the Bible: "Wives, submit to your husbands...." We didn't agree on this subject. Because of my previous relationships, "submission" had become a bad word to me. I believed that if Kevin loved me "as Christ loved the church" (as instructed in Ephesians 5:25), then we would have no issues. I wondered if I could really be submissive to a man; after all, I was now an independent career woman capably caring for myself and my daughters. I wondered if Kevin really could love me as Jesus loved the church. Kevin reassured me that this topic wouldn't be a problem in our marriage; he was certain that God intended us to be together and confident that, as we trusted Him, our marriage would flourish. Kevin continued writing me tender love letters that encouraged me about the promise of our future together.

Besides being a youth counselor for the church, Kevin was also the bass player in the youth-church's rock-n-roll band, Ian's Dream. In September, we traveled on a mission trip to Russia. Kevin toured with the band as I performed in drama skits. Communism in Russia was crumbling and missionaries from every denomination were there, sharing the Gospel. Calvary Chapel Downey had started a church in Vladimir, Russia, where we performed concerts and drama skits to help evangelize the Russian communities and encourage the local believers.

~

I realized third-world countries didn't need modernization; they needed Jesus.

~

Growing up, I was taught that Russia was a powerful enemy, so when I arrived I expected to encounter a thriving superpower. I was shocked to discover, instead, a third-world country. Everyone kept their heads down, stoically avoiding eye contact. What a joy to witness the oppression of communism fall off of people—as if they were discarding an old coat—when they went forward during our gospel presentations and accepted Jesus as their Lord and Savior. People were smiling, laughing, and following us around like we were movie stars. Our pastor kept reminding them we were just vessels delivering the message of Jesus to their country.

This was a phenomenal experience, as God opened my eyes to see the world from a different perspective. I realized that third-world countries didn't need modernization; they needed Jesus. I remember one night after our drama skit, Pastor Jeff gave an altar call and dozens of Russian men, dressed in military uniforms, publicly invited Jesus into their hearts. As they were coming forward, I saw God instantly transform tough, emotionally detached, criminal enforcers into tearful broken men who were seizing a relationship with Jesus.

When we returned from the trip in September, I continued commuting from Whittier to Bakersfield, as I'd been doing since before going to Russia, since it was my job to oversee Security Signal's acquisition of Kern Security. During one of my commutes to Bakersfield, Kevin brought the girls with him from Whittier to visit me and take all of us to the Kern County Fair. At the end of the night, we wanted to spend the night together, but Kevin had to take the girls back to Whittier for school the next day. In addition, we wanted to honor our understanding of Hebrews 13:4 in the Bible, which instructs couples to wait until marriage to become physically intimate. It was hard to watch him leave. As he said goodbye, he told me to play track six on the Beach Boys soundtrack—"Wouldn't it Be Nice." As I listened, I realized Kevin was reading my mind:

> You know its gonna make it that much better
> When we can say good-night and stay together
> Wouldn't it be nice if we could wake up
> In the morning, when the day is new?
> And after having spent the day together
> Hold each other close the whole night through
> Happy times together we've been spending
> I wish that every kiss was never ending
> Oh, wouldn't it be nice?[3]

The geographical distance, added to the angst of leaving one another every night, was tough on our new relationship and continued to weigh heavily on us. Even so, Kevin and I had plans for a big church wedding in November and we were very excited about our future together.

Shortly after the fair, Kevin and I dropped my mom off at the airport to visit her boyfriend and his family and, at the last minute, decided to hop on a plane to Las Vegas and elope. Our plan was to keep our November wedding arrangements in place so we could get

---

[3] Brian Wilson, Tony Asher, Mike Love, "Wouldn't it Be Nice," Capitol Records, 1966.

married in our home church six weeks later and celebrate our love with friends, family, and other loved ones. We told no one, not even my maid of honor.

As newlyweds, Kevin and I began spending our nights together at my apartment. However, when a neighbor, who attended our church, told our pastor that Kevin was staying at my place, the church leaders confronted Kevin. Kevin explained that we were spending the night together because we had eloped. This set off a chain reaction among our church leaders, who debated whether to allow us to get married in November in the church. We were devastated. With the wedding only weeks away, I had purchased my gown and everything was set for the ceremony. I called our Senior Pastor, Jeff, to share my heart on why we eloped. He told me he would discuss our conversation with the church leaders and get back to me. A couple of days later, Pastor Jeff called to say the wedding would move forward. Kevin and I felt relieved, grateful, and excited. My dream wedding was to be married in the same church where we first met and ministered together.

It seemed like many obstacles were coming against our church wedding, but we felt like, in the tough battles, we were victorious. That is, until Kevin and I went to pick up his son for Thanksgiving and the wedding. When we arrived at the house, there was a note on the door from Child Protective Services ordering Kevin not to take him. The note said to expect a future hearing regarding trumped-up allegations that one of Kevin's family members had sexually molested his son. We were certain the charges were false, and we were furious. I had no idea this was the beginning of a battle that would last for many years.

Kevin's parents hosted Thanksgiving dinner and we invited both sides of our families. This was the first time we'd had everyone together under one roof. It was nice that we didn't have to cook and could enjoy getting to know each other's family members before our wedding.

Two days later, on November 27, 1993, Kevin and I celebrated our wedding ceremony at Calvary Chapel Downey. It was amazing. Church friends, the youth group, our bridal party, and all our friends and family were there—over 300 people. Everything was perfect. We played a brand-new song by Dan Marks, titled "For Me and My House." I felt so much peace that day. All the stresses of the wedding, court hearings for custody, nearly canceling the entire ceremony, flowers not arriving on time, and decorations being finalized as I was walking down the aisle, didn't matter to me. I was present in the moment and in awe that our big day had finally arrived. I'd ordered three dozen white roses for my bouquet and was enamored with their beauty. I'll never forget, when the sanctuary doors opened, seeing Kevin—handsome and clean cut—standing at the altar with tears in his eyes. The ceremony was exactly everything I'd ever dreamed of, including incorporating our kids into it to blend our families together.

The next morning at 5 a.m. sharp, Kevin's best man, Rick, picked us up and took us to the airport for our honeymoon—a week in Puerto Rico followed by a week-long cruise to the Virgin Islands. It was spectacular! The Virgin Islands were decked out with Christmas trees and decorations. It was the perfect transition— from the wedding ceremony, to the reception, to the honeymoon, to the excitement of celebrating our first Christmas together. The first night of our honeymoon, Kevin and I exchanged gifts. Kevin's special gift to me was a blue leather-bound Bible with my name, Deborah Ann Ormonde, engraved on it. God not only replaced my prize, but He gave me a new name and a new foundation. The little girl who'd closed her heart for business so many years ago was now revived with hope, love, and dreams of a positive future.

Chapter 12

Tragic Years

"Stress is an intrusion on your peaceful existence.
All of us strive to have orderly and peaceful lives."
— Healthstatus.com

HealthStatus, a health-risk assessment provider, lists the top-five most stressful life events as follows: the death of a loved one, divorce, moving, major illness, and job loss. For me, 2006 was a tragic and stressful year as I dealt with four out of life's five top stressors. On the outside, everything looked put together, but on the inside, everything was falling apart. I felt like something was missing and my life was one big pressure cooker waiting to explode.

I was taking on the identity of a Chameleon Christian, and there was no way I would let anyone know what was really going on in our lives. Being in children's ministry for 14 years, working as an executive leader, and having a family that was very involved in ministry, we dared not talk about all the stressors we faced. People needed us to have it together, so we maintained the mask that we did have it all together … and we did a good job at it, too.

My career was doing well. I was the Vice President of Kern, one of the top-20 security companies in the United States. Kevin and I experienced the typical issues that couples with blended families face. Lisa had married her college-church-group sweetheart in 2001. Kevin's oldest son, Joshua, got married in 2004 while Devin continued to live with his biological mother in Southern California. Amy moved out on her own around 2003 and Kevin and I had two children together, Levi, 9, and Hope, 7.

Kevin and I sold our house during the 2006 housing boom. Within three days of listing our home, it sold with a 30-day escrow. We had to move and had no place to go so, we moved into our "fifth wheel" travel trailer for about two months before purchasing our new home. I'd become concerned about my 72-year-old mother's cognitive and health status and began questioning whether our lives were really as "together" as they appeared to outsiders.

In April, I received a 5 a.m. phone call from the Transportation Security Administration. They'd found my mother wandering in the back of Meadows Field Airport. When Kevin and I arrived at the airport, we questioned my mom about why she was there and what she was doing. Her story was very confusing and involved people who were nowhere to be found. Mother claimed strangers had shown up at her home that morning—people she'd invited inside, entertained, cooked breakfast for, and driven to the airport. As soon as she arrived, they jumped out of the car, hopped the fence, and ran off.

Feeling frustrated, I drove her home, hoping that its condition might shed some light on her story. It didn't. Everything was in order. The house was clean, the beds were made, and everything was in its place, except for a frying pan she'd placed on the linoleum countertop, scorching the surface.

I called her doctor that same day and told him I was concerned about my mom's mental state. He said I needed to confiscate either her car keys or her medication until she could be evaluated and tested. However, there was absolutely no way my mother was going to voluntarily part with either of these essential items. From as early as I can remember, my mom was addicted to opioids. When she transitioned from illegal drugs to prescription drugs, her dealers went from selling drugs at the local street corner to dispensing them in nice office buildings.

~

Kevin was dumbfounded that Mother would allow me to go to jail over her drug abuse.

~

When I told my mom her options, she flipped out, just as I'd anticipated. I couldn't find her car keys, but I knew from my childhood experience where she stashed her pills. Grabbing a box, I began opening cupboards, coffee cans, oven mitts, and closets, and searching under her bed and in various other spots. I filled the entire box with bottles of 120 pills each. There were thousands of pills. I took these pills back to my office and had my assistant catalog what the medications were, how many pills were in each bottle, which doctor wrote the prescription, and the pharmacy that filled it.

Within hours of leaving her house, I received a phone call from the Bakersfield police department telling me to return the pills to mom's house or they would arrest me for stealing her medications. I printed my list of medications and documents she'd signed years earlier, listing me as having power of attorney for her. By the time I arrived, the police, Kevin, Levi, and Hope were already on the scene. To the police, my mom's allegations seemed completely legitimate so, at first, they treated me like a pill thief and interrogated me for

25 minutes in preparation for my arrest. When I told them I had power of attorney and showed them the list of medications, my mom screamed and yelled that I was lying. The police reviewed the documents and realized she was actually the one not telling the truth and they let me go.

Kevin was dumbfounded that Mother would allow me to go to jail over her drug abuse. He stated unequivocally that he'd had enough of my mom's recklessness. She could no longer come over or spend time with our kids. Sure enough, when my mom dropped by the following Easter to give Easter baskets to the kids, Kevin wouldn't let her in the house. After we argued over him making her sit outside, I took the kids outside to see Mom and thank her for their gifts.

Although I was angry with Kevin's decision and the friction was starting to take a toll on our marriage, I learned more about healthy boundaries through a Bible study with a friend over the next few months. Looking back, these were the first steps toward learning to embrace radical obedience to Jesus.

In June of that same year, my mother ran a red light and t-boned an 18-wheeler truck, breaking her leg in several places. At the hospital, pins were inserted into her leg and traction helped stabilize, straighten, and immobilize her shattered limb. Mom never lived by herself again after the accident. After a three-week hospital stay, she moved into a rehabilitation center to start physical therapy so she could learn to walk again. However, she refused to do the work necessary to regain her mobility and seemed mad at the world. I moved her into an assisted living home after four months.

Tragedy struck my family once again on July 17th, when my sister-in-law, Nancy, called from Indiana crying so hysterically that I couldn't understand what she was trying to tell me. "She's gone, she's gone," she wailed. Finally, she caught her breath long enough to tell me that my niece—Steven and Nancy's daughter, Rebekah—was "gone." I didn't understand. What was Nancy talking about? Was Rebekah missing? Had she run away? What I heard next almost stopped my heart. Seventeen-year-old Rebekah had been executed in a cornfield.

~

I realized I'd been living in survival mode when God wanted me to live in surrender mode.

~

Police reports said she'd gone out that evening with four other kids, crossing through a cornfield to hang out near a stream. Suddenly, one of the five pulled out an AR-15 rifle and shot the other four. Three were killed and one survived. The horrific event launched a two-week manhunt in Indiana for the killer. The story was aired on "America's Most Wanted" and the assailant was eventually arrested.

A week after that tragic phone call, I attended Rebekah's funeral. It was a hot, humid morning in Evansville, Indiana. The service was packed with friends and loved ones. Memories and quotes, handwritten on colorful bandanas, lined the casket where my beautiful niece lay motionless and pale. It was completely surreal. Nancy sobbed uncontrollably and asked me to view Rebekah's body. The ten minutes I spent in front of her open casket felt like an eternity. As I grieved at the gravesite, watching them lower Rebekah's coffin into the ground, my phone vibrated. My daughter, Lisa, messaged me that my granddaughter, Emma, had just been born. My heart was torn between grieving the loss of one precious young life and rejoicing over the birth of another. I returned home the next morning.

Mother's erratic behavior, it turned out, was caused by the

ravages of Alzheimer's disease. As her physical condition continued to deteriorate daily, she tried using a walker but found the experience too frustrating. Wheelchair-bound, she continued to refuse physical therapy, wouldn't cooperate with the staff, and was constantly in trouble because of her hostile, combative behavior with everyone. The staff couldn't handle her and, at their request, I moved her for a third time to a new facility.

My world was caving in and Kevin didn't understand how to help, what to say, or what to do. Instead of stepping up to support and assist me, I felt like he took a step back. Totally disconnected, one day we had an argument at work and I became so angry that I stormed out of his office, slammed the door, and walked into my office. My new assistant, Nikki, came in to make sure I was alright. As soon as she left, I noticed my kids' pictures on the wall and heard God speak to my heart: "You are at a crossroads in your life and must decide which path you will take."

I had known Jesus since I was a little girl, riding the bus to church each Sunday. But it was in this moment that I realized I'd been living in survival mode when God wanted me to live in surrender mode. It was time to make a choice. Was I going to continue trying to manage my life as best I could or trust God to do it? I cried out to God about my marriage, my family, and my relationship with Jesus. This was war, and I was preparing for the biggest battle of my life—a battle with Satan to free the prisoner from within.

Desperately in need of wise counsel, I made an appointment to see my pastor. I went there by myself and explained how everything in my life was going wrong. Without explanation, Pastor Mike stopped me, mid-sentence, and asked me about my childhood. I looked at him like he was crazy. Why in the world, at a time like this, did he want to talk about my past? Didn't he understand? I'm in crisis here!

Unfazed, he told me we *were* going to talk about my childhood. "No!" I protested. And, with that, he calmly picked up a book and started reading. It was as if he was waiting on me, and we had all day. Each time I stubbornly began to talk about my current problems, Pastor Mike refused to indulge me. We sat there in silence for more than half an hour—the longest 35 minutes of my life. Then, he calmy told me my time was up, ushered me out of his office, and asked if I'd like to return for another session. I don't know who was more surprised by the "yes" that came out of my mouth, him or me. But my situation was desperate. I knew I needed help.

When I returned the next week, I immediately began recounting everything that was going wrong in my world. And, once again, my pastor stopped me in my tracks. He said he didn't want to hear about any of this; he wanted to hear about my childhood. I explained that my childhood had nothing whatsoever to do with my current life issues. Clearly, my problem was my marriage, work, children, and stress. He said we would talk about all of these issues at another time. But, today, he wanted to talk about my childhood. Again, I refused. And, again, he picked up a book and began reading. *What a jerk!* I thought, outraged to be put on the spot. I couldn't talk to him about my childhood. I was a ministry leader and an executive at a large corporation. There was no way I could let him into my past. I couldn't believe he was just sitting there reading his stupid book. At the end of the hour, he again told me my time was up. And, once again, he asked if I wanted to come back. Again, I said "Yes!" I didn't know what was happening, but something was drawing me back to meet with him.

At the beginning of our third appointment, we repeated the same exact process. I started talking about my current problems, only to be interrupted and asked about my childhood. This time, I told him, "Listen, Pastor Mike, I haven't discussed my childhood with anyone. It's been safely tucked away my entire life." Besides, even if I were to talk about it, I didn't even know where to begin. He responded by asking me to tell him about happy and sad times in my childhood. I began to open up slowly. Then, it was like the floodgates released. We far exceeded our hour-long session that day. Toward the end, he asked me if I would be willing to begin sharing my past with Kevin. I asked him why, after 17 years of marriage, I should consider doing so. He explained that my present pain was directly tied to my past experiences. I was angry because of the burdens I'd been secretly shouldering and I was seeing my life through the eyes of a hurt, abandoned child.

I didn't realize this was even a possibility until Pastor Mike revealed it to me. Life had taught me that people weren't to be trusted. But God had a different plan. He was done with my masks, my secrets, and my pretending. He wouldn't allow me to continue living life the way I wanted and still call myself a Christian. Doing otherwise would make Him a liar.

Chapter 13

Diagnosis

"The Lord is close to the brokenhearted and
saves those who are crushed in spirit."
— Psalm 34:18 (NIV)

On New Year's Eve of 2008, I was celebrating at Hume Lake Christian Camp with Kevin, Levi, and Hope, blissfully unplugged from the world. A big dinner was served, pizzas and cookies were baked, and servers were dancing, joyfully dishing out these treats to the crowd. A new year was approaching, and we were excited about what it would bring. As the countdown to midnight began, kids screamed in sheer exhilaration and, at the stroke of midnight, a net above our heads released hundreds of balloons as we rejoiced in the hope of a new year. After everything settled down, we grabbed a few cookies to go, donned our coats, and headed to our cabin, looking forward to a good night's rest and the beginning of 2009.

Our cabin was nicely appointed, warm, and cozy. Everyone had settled into their beds when, around 12:30 a.m., I heard a knock.

Thinking someone was at the wrong cabin, I answered the door and was greeted by a young woman named Julie, whom I'd gotten to know casually while here on our vacation at the camp. But when I saw her despairing face, I knew something was terribly wrong. Julie told me that my daughter, Lisa, was on the phone with an emergency. She said that they had taken my granddaughter to the hospital.

~

Unable, or possibly even unwilling, to acknowledge the magnitude of the diagnosis, it took me months to come to grips with the unthinkable implications.

~

It was icy and cold outside and I was in shock as we carefully maneuvered toward Julie's golf cart, which was parked down a steep hill. Once inside, Julie told me to hold on and she took off, driving as fast as she could to the lodge. There, I rushed to the old landline, which was off the receiver when I picked it up. Lisa was on the line and told me that Emma, my granddaughter, had been taken by ambulance to the Children's Hospital in Madera following a rectal prolapse. Tearfully, Lisa explained that, when she'd removed Emma's diaper for a routine change, to her utter shock, the diaper contained her baby's rectum—the last several inches of the large intestine, closest to the anus. Though testing was needed to confirm a diagnosis, doctors told Lisa that Emma might have Cystic Fibrosis, a genetic disorder that causes severe organ damage. More testing was needed, which is why Emma had been transferred by ambulance from Bakersfield to Madera Children's Hospital.

When Lisa told me that the illness is genetic and terminal, with no potential cure, I could barely comprehend the words. I didn't know anything about the disease or what it all meant. I continued to listen to Lisa, trying desperately to console her. Surely, it was nothing too serious. Surely, the doctors could handle whatever the problem was. Surely, we would get answers to remedy the situation. After the phone call, I returned to the cabin, prayed, and tried to rest for a few hours. Then, we packed and started the nearly two-hour drive to the hospital. When we arrived, Emma's diagnosis was still unconfirmed. In shock and denial, I felt confident that doctors would tell Lisa it was all going to be okay and send them home, where Emma would eventually recover.

Instead, on January 2, 2008, Lisa called to confirm that our precious Emma did, in fact, have Cystic Fibrosis. Unable, or possibly even unwilling, to acknowledge the magnitude of the diagnosis, it took me months to come to grips with the unthinkable implications. And so began a journey that would take my relationship with God deeper than I'd ever thought possible—a journey that led me to embrace the reality of Psalm 34:18: "The Lord is close to the brokenhearted and saves those who are crushed in spirit."

During the first year of Emma's diagnosis, the South-central California community of Taft held a Fall fair to raise money for her medical care. Around Christmas, the Chevron corporation adopted Lisa's family and showered them with gifts. It was amazing to see the community stepping in and loving them. I must admit that accepting help from others was hard and embarrassing for me. I believed it was Kevin's and my responsibility to handle this enormous financial and emotional burden all by ourselves. I gradually learned, however, that this misguided belief was my pride talking. God was showing me the importance of letting the church community step in and help in times of crisis.[4] As they did, He was also showing me how to trust Him. When insurance wouldn't cover medical needs, miraculous

---

[4] See Philippians 2:4, Galatians 6:2, Luke 6:38, and Hebrews 13:16, for examples.

things would happen and Emma's needs were continuously met. God was teaching me He would take care of Lisa and her family— and that doing so was, first and foremost, His job, not mine.

Chapter 14

Growing up

For Christmas of 2008, like so many Christmases before, I received a gift from my oldest childhood friend, Reggie. Only this year's gift was unlike anything I'd ever imagined. In fact, my first impulse was to send it back. You see, this year's gift was a GED preparation book. I tossed the book to the side and thought, *What the heck is he thinking?* Inside, was a card with a note that read, "You need to do this for you."

With thinly disguised exasperation, I called Reggie and reminded him that I was the Vice President of a well-known security company and that, at this stage of my life and career, I had absolutely no need for a high school equivalency diploma. What I didn't tell him was that I was secretly insecure about my ability to obtain my GED. After dropping out of school at the beginning of seventh grade, I'd never completed anything. Everything I'd ever started I would drop.

Though I wasn't sure of exactly why, over time, I began researching what it would take to start my GED. Simultaneously, my mind raced to the possibilities of obtaining a higher education. If I were to return to school, I didn't want to be limited by a GED alone.

~

I began wondering how I could diplomatically get out of the situation without having to tell Donna the truth about why I was in her office.

~

One morning, I drove to Bakersfield Adult School dressed in a business suit and asked to meet with a counselor. They didn't know I was coming to enroll as a student and assumed I was there for an appointment with an administration member. I told them I wanted to discuss earning my high school diploma. They asked me how many credits I had from high school. I told them I had none. They were shocked.

The counselor took me to her boss, who tried to talk me out of completing my high school diploma. They said I should work on my GED instead. I told them I didn't want to do that because I wanted to be able to accept a diploma wearing a cap and gown. She explained that earning an actual diploma would be time-consuming and require me to take a lot of elective courses like computer lab, sewing, and many others. I told her that if I got my GED, I would be limited and wouldn't be able to achieve my next academic goal of transferring to Cal State Bakersfield. She called Cal State, placed the academic advisor on speakerphone, and asked him, if I finished my GED, whether the college would accept me. The advisor said they most certainly would. After the call, I told the counselor, "I don't know anything about algebra, but I can do payroll, run financial reports, and do anything that has to do with business math." She assured me I could do high school math and gave me the contact information for the local literacy center, which offered a free tutor. I enrolled for a test date for my GED.

The next day, I went to the Kern Literacy Center, only to see Kern Security signs all over the building. I immediately thought, *There is just no way I can do this. Kern Literacy Center is my company's client!* Fearing humiliation, I forced myself to go inside, where I told the friendly receptionist I was there to find a math tutor to help prepare me for my GED. She took my information back to the Center's Executive Director, Donna, who soon called me into her office. There, she told me how she knew me and how marvelous I was. She recounted a story of how we had installed the Center's security system for free. Donna, it seemed, had been in the market for a security system when she came across a news article that featured me. After reading it, she ran into one of our service technicians and asked who she needed to speak with to have a system installed for a nonprofit. The service technician gave her my name and number, which she called, bypassing the receptionist and speaking directly with me. Though I hadn't remembered it until she recounted the story, I'd offered to have our company install her system for free.

As she was telling me her story, I started to feel embarrassed and uncomfortable. I began wondering how I could diplomatically get out of the situation without having to tell Donna the truth about why I was in her office. Before I could hatch a plan, though, Donna stopped telling me her story and asked me what I needed. Cornered, I blurted out that I needed an algebra tutor. To my surprise, she was completely gracious and unfazed. In fact, she said she had the perfect person in mind—their star tutor.

The day I went to meet my tutor, in walked my son's friend's grandfather from Stockdale Christian School. I was mortified. I knew him and wondered what everyone at the school would think about me once they found out about my educational shortcomings. After sharing my story, though, he was nothing but compassionate and eager to help me. Fear could have stopped me from doing what I was supposed to do, but it didn't. I began secretly to tutor with him after work, three days a week, for about two months. Always incredibly supportive, he called me the morning of my test to cheer me on. After three short months of study, I passed my GED!

I felt extremely excited and proud of my accomplishment and immediately called Reggie to share the great news. My biggest fan and cheerleader, he was so thrilled that, for my graduation present, he flew my family to Boston. We had a great time there sightseeing, then drove up to Maine, where we enjoyed a spectacular week.

After completing my GED in early 2008, I enrolled in Summit Bible College's Bachelor/Master Concurrent program. I graduated in June 2011 with my Bachelor of Leadership and Master of Biblical Counseling. Four years later, I earned my Doctor of Divinity. After 43 years, I was no longer bound by my limited education!

Chapter 15

Back to the Beginning

"He has made everything beautiful in its time.
He has also set eternity in the human heart; yet no one can
fathom what God has done from the beginning to the end."
— Ecclesiastes 3:11 (NIV)

For years, I'd been involved in children's ministry, which I loved and enjoyed. It was safe, comfortable, and easy. Nonetheless, in 2008, I started to become restless and sensed a strong desire to start working with juvenile delinquents. I understood very well how quickly a life could be taken. It was a frightening reality. I knew there was a need to help young teens learn their purpose and identity in the world. My granddaughter Emma's terminal diagnosis, which broke my heart, also spurred deep soul-searching. I needed to know my own purpose in life.

As I struggled with internal restlessness, I felt I needed to step out of my comfort zone. I considered working with women in prison, but I didn't feel ready for that. I prayed for God to lead me where he wanted me to go. Then one day, while driving down California Avenue, I passed Bakersfield High School, looked to my left, and saw the "Youth for Christ" building. Instantly, the Holy Spirit told me to stop there. I stubbornly kept driving. As I did, my thoughts were flooded with memories from my days in juvenile hall and the book I'd read there, *The Cross and the Switchblade*. While arguing with God and feeling frustrated, I realized I had an opportunity to move over to the turn left lane and make a U-turn. At the very last moment, I did. Heading back to the Youth for Christ building, I gave God a list of conditions He'd have to meet if I was to go in there. First, I needed more clarity and complete assurance that He wanted me to do this. Next, I told God He had to make this an easy task for me and that, if the staff wouldn't meet with me, were rude, or if I had any doubts, I would turn right around and leave.

~

Afraid and uncertain, I thought I would have absolutely nothing in common with these girls....

~

Everyone at Youth for Christ was incredibly friendly, welcoming, and courteous. We met and talked and I shared a bit of my story. Three hours later, I was signed up as a new volunteer, assigned to teach classes at the local juvenile hall.

Four teenage girls awaited me in my first class at the all-girl facility, where I was joined by another volunteer who wanted to observe my teaching style. It had been years since I'd been around juvenile delinquents. I had spent most of my adult life around successful business people. I taught from the program "Life Hurts, God Heals," a curriculum I bought from Saddleback Church.

Afraid and uncertain, I thought I would have absolutely nothing in common with these girls and was unsure of how they would respond. But in talking with them and hearing their stories, it reminded me of my own life and we had an unexpected, almost-instant connection. After that first night, I was hooked! Quickly, my teaching became the highlight of my week. Every day before class, I concentrated on how I could help these girls deal with their problems. When I was at work, my heart was focused on them. I couldn't wait to be in front of them again. I was hungry to give them more of my time, energy, and focus.

During our classes, my students would always talk about their BFFs, which stood for "best friend forever." The girls used this acronym so often that I knew, one day, I would re-purpose it. In 2008, I opened a nonprofit to mentor juveniles. Its name: Be Finally Free, Inc.

Chapter 16

Liberia 2008

"When wounds are healed by love,
the scars are beautiful."
— David Bowles

During my journey to discover my life's purpose, I opened my heart to new opportunities to seek God's will for my life. Upon reading many of Kevin's amazing journal entries and letters about his personal experiences on mission trips to Liberia, I was intrigued and wanted to experience it for myself. Kevin had been to Africa seven or eight times and, when he planned another trip to visit Ghana and Liberia in West Africa, I decided to join him. He was scheduled to speak several times in Ghana and we were each scheduled to speak, in separate churches, afterward in Liberia. Kevin warned me there was no way to prepare my message after arriving in Africa, so I prepared a message before we left.

Upon arriving in Ghana, we stayed at a beautiful retreat center overnight to rest and recover from jet lag. Although we toured non-stop, staying in Ghana was like a vacation for me. I felt comfortable there; they had convenient amenities, stores, restaurants, and hotels. It was like visiting a U.S. city.

I was excited and amazed to watch Kevin speak at different churches during the various leadership conferences we attended. He was on fire, breathing life into the conference attendees. He was funny, entertaining, and the Spirit of God was clearly moving in these places. I sat in the front row each time he spoke, stunned to see him operating in his anointing. It was remarkable! I was mesmerized and in awe of my husband, and it got better everywhere we went.

~

I couldn't expect to walk into my destiny while continuing to live with all the lies.

~

Along the way, we got to enjoy some sightseeing, including a jungle "canopy walk" and a visit to a slave castle—a haunting fortress where, hundreds of years prior, slaves were held before being loaded onto ships bound for the Americas. I learned so much about the history of West Africa as God was showing me how to love people from all walks of life.

Finally, we left for Liberia, the place Kevin called his beloved. On the plane, I read *A Long Way Gone, Memoirs of a Boy Soldier* by Ishmael Beah, a heartbreaking story of how rebels in Sierra Leone captured young children and forced them to fight as soldiers. During the civil war, these innocent children were tortured, punished, and brainwashed to attack anyone and everything while fighting on the front lines.

When we arrived, it was pitch black. As our hosts, Daniel and Pastor Brown, drove us through the dark jungle toward our destination, the only lights I could see flickered dimly inside candle-lit huts. I couldn't stop thinking of the book I'd just read and how, between 1991 and 2002, tens of thousands of young soldier-boys lived in the African jungle, battling enemies, the elements, and their own tormented thoughts.

I was exhausted when we arrived at our guest house and fell into bed. The next morning, as I prepared to shower, I was greeted by a tarantula the size of my hand as I pushed back the shower curtain. Kevin heroically killed it as I cowered nearby. Relieved, I returned to the bathroom, only to discover another giant tarantula on the back of the door. Not wanting to over-react, complain, or be a burden, I committed to doing my best to stay focused on the mission and downplay the distractions. However, that night, while lying in bed, I noticed a hole in the ceiling directly above our bed. All I could think about was another tarantula creeping out of it at the exact moment I closed my eyes. I was terrified. I can't remember if or how I got to sleep that night.

The next morning, we went out to explore the surrounding area and I was shocked to see how Liberian villagers lived. Atrocities and destruction from the war were everywhere. No amount of reading could have prepared me for what I saw. We traveled to a farm that Kevin had been raising money for during his many mission trips back and forth to Liberia. Just when I thought things couldn't get worse than showering and sleeping with tarantulas, we blew past a security checkpoint, and Liberian police instantly descended on us with guns. The pastors jumped out of our car and yelled at the officers. Horrified, I asked Kevin what was going on, envisioning my imminent involvement in a gruesome scene like one I'd read about in the book.

Mayhem ensued as opposing parties yelled back and forth. *NO! Don't yell at police with guns pointing at us*, I screamed silently. Kevin, who stayed in the car with me, told me not to worry, assuring me that this was the normal way disputes were resolved in the region. *Oh, swell!* By the time the pastors got back in the car, untroubled and laughing about the situation, I was a wreck. To me, there was nothing funny about it. We proceeded to the farm and, that night, were moved to a hotel that was, I'm pleased to report, tarantula-free.

Before coming to Africa, I had prepared a message about suffering. But during my short stay in Liberia, I realized that nothing I had endured could compare with the inhumane things these people had experienced. I could teach them nothing about suffering. At the hotel, I tried to put together a message and, finally, waved my Bible in frustration, crying out to God, "What am I supposed to do with this? I need help." I was mad at God. I had no message, no way to prepare a message, no Bible commentary, no curriculum. I felt completely unqualified. I was forced to rely on the Bible as my only resource. At the time, I didn't realize it was all I ever needed.

The Holy Spirit kept prompting me, "Tell them your story." I didn't want to tell my story. Except for Pastor Mike and Kevin, I had told no one my story, and I hadn't even told Kevin until 17 years after we married. I felt overwhelmed, like I wanted to run, when the Holy Spirit spoke to me: "I brought you halfway around the world so you could feel safe to tell your story; now tell it!"

I wrote a few notes about my story on a piece of paper shortly before I was picked up to speak at the church near Monrovia, Liberia's capital city. Upon arriving, the music was loud and everyone was dancing. The environment was electrifying. People were dressed in bright, vivid colors and everyone was so friendly and welcoming. They seated me in the front of the church as sweat poured down the front of my shirt because I was so nervous, and it was hot and humid. As I watched everyone dance, I felt out of place. Meanwhile, ideas about what to say raced through my head. I remembered a story about a football player from 25 years ago, Miles McPherson, who was scheduled to speak at an elementary school. They'd decked the whole place out and everyone was cheering for him. But he was so nervous that, upon taking the mic, he sputtered, "Hi, my name is Miles McPherson. Be cool and stay in school." Then he walked off. This was exactly what I felt like I was going to do. I was scheduled to speak for an hour, yet I had only a few scribbled notes.

After a kind introduction, I stepped up on the stage and shared a 15-minute portion of my story. As I spoke, I felt my spiritual and emotional chains falling off. I knew, without a shadow of a doubt, that the baggage from my past had been holding me back. I couldn't expect to walk into my destiny while continuing to live with all the lies. It was the first time I had ever shared a portion of my story publicly. Unbeknownst to me, a reporter was in the audience that day. He shared my story on the front page of the Monrovia newspaper, The Informer. I believe this happened so God could show me that, if I obeyed and told my story, He would give me the words I needed to say. "For the Holy Spirit will teach you in that very hour what you ought to say" (Luke 12:12, ESV).

Kevin and I flew home three days after arriving in Liberia. Even though God had orchestrated a dramatic breakthrough in my life during my visit to this war-torn country, I was still determined never to return to Liberia because of the hardships of foreign travel. I told Kevin on the plane that God would have to speak to me audibly before I ever returned to this place.

Chapter 17

Saying Good-Bye

*"There are special people in our lives who never leave us ...
even after they are gone."*
– Unknown

A round November of 2010, I moved my mother into a new assisted-living home, confident that this was the right place for her. It was nice and clean, the environment was pleasant, they offered numerous activities, and the staff took good care of her. Nevertheless, she was combative and her Alzheimer's continued to worsen.

The following month, I received a call about my mom. As had been the case before, I was asked to move her because the staff couldn't handle her. I was crestfallen. Having finally found a good place for her, I'd need to uproot her yet again. I looked at new facilities and smaller homes, but nothing was a good fit. I was out of options. At this point, I was upset with my mom, my husband, my siblings—who weren't helping—my kids, and with God. Truth be told, I was downright angry. It seemed unfair that the burden for

107

mom's care was falling entirely on my shoulders. I wanted relief and help, but no one stepped up. My mother was placed in hospice care three times during this period, yet she would always bounce back. She never fully recovered, which made it more difficult for me to bear the burden of helping her single-handedly.

~

If beauty ever was present in the midst of death,
it was in that moment.

~

On January 14, 2011, I was attending my daughter, Hope's, spelling bee and had to silence my phone. Hope was told to spell "edition" but, because she didn't ask for the definition, she spelled "addition" instead. After being disqualified, she was upset and we left the building right away. While checking to see if I had missed any calls or messages, my phone vibrated and I answered it. The nurse at my mother's assisted living home told me Mom's oxygen levels were at 16 (normal is 75 to 100) and they wanted to transfer her to the hospital. My mom had signed a "do not resuscitate" order, though, and I had to make the hardest decision of my life. I told the staff not to transfer her. I knew it was time to let her go.

We left the spelling bee and went straight to the assisted living home. My daughters, Amy and Lisa; Lisa's husband, Matt; and Kevin met me there. Kevin held my mother's hand and prayed over her while Matt softly played worship music on his guitar. Within an hour and a half, she passed on. If beauty ever was present in the midst of death, it was in that moment.

Fortunately, I'd made funeral arrangements prior to my mother's death. The memorial services were beautiful. Kevin officiated her funeral and my brother, Steven, delivered the eulogy. Matt played "Simple Man" by Lynyrd Skynyrd on the guitar, a song Steven had selected, along with some worship music. I believed my mom would have been extremely proud of how she was honored. That same day, we held another service for her in Riverside, California. Afterward, she was laid to rest at Riverside National Cemetery next to my dad.

Chapter 18

The Road to Freedom

"I imagine one of the reasons people cling to their hates so stubbornly is because they sense once hate is gone, they will be forced to deal with pain."
— James Baldwin

After my mom's death, I was working at Kern Security, developing Be Finally Free, and mentoring juveniles. As I poured myself into pursuing the ministry vision God was giving me, I was feeling the call to leave my job in the security industry and do ministry full-time. Against this backdrop, I was invited to speak at Lerdo jail in Bakersfield. On my first visit, I knew immediately that I was called to work with incarcerated men and women. I was able to relate and communicate differently with them and, through the ministry, I saw God transform their lives.

One night, I was speaking to the women at Lerdo on the topic of forgiveness. As I was leaving the jail afterward, I had a full-on encounter with the Holy Spirit.

Holy Spirit: *What about you?*

Me: *What about me? What are you talking about?*

Holy Spirit: *What about forgiving and sharing the Gospel with Nick?*

Me: *NO WAY! What about the pain it will cause my brother if I reach out to the man who murdered his daughter? I can't do this!*

My conversation with the Holy Spirit ended as abruptly as it began and, from that night on, I couldn't stop thinking about Nicholas Harbison, my niece, Rebekah's, convicted killer. Morning, noon, and night he came to mind. I even told Kevin that I thought I needed to see a psychiatrist because I could *not* get Nick out of my head.

~

I heard the Holy Spirit ask me, "What if you could never have another bean-and-cheese burrito in your life?"
I knew exactly what He meant.

~

I'd wake up thinking about this heinous killer. I'd go to work thinking about him. I'd go to sleep thinking about him. But, all the while, God was stirring my heart about more than just forgiveness. It was about obedience, total surrender, and doing what God asked me to do, no matter the cost, whether or not it made any sense to me.

One day, in the Taco Bell drive-thru, I placed my order for a bean-and-cheese burrito, then drove up to the window to pay. At that moment, I heard the Holy Spirit ask me, "What if you could never have another bean-and-cheese burrito in your life?" I knew exactly what He meant. God was reminding me of Nick's plight, locked behind bars without access to the fast food I took for granted. Wrestling with God was emotionally draining and exhausting. I felt like I was losing my mind. There in my car, I threw my hands in the air and yelled out to God, "I don't care!"

Eventually, however, God, prevailed. I wrote Nick a five-page letter and shared the Gospel with him. At that point, Nick had been in prison for five years. He was serving three consecutive life sentences plus 50 years. The letter read:

> My prayer for me has been that I could truly forgive you for the hurt, pain, and devastation you caused my family and the White and Lynch families. God continually has placed you on my heart and I have thought about you at the craziest times. I knew that I needed to forgive your actions.
>
> Forgiveness is not about ignoring evil, excusing it, or making light of it. On the contrary, forgiveness courageously faces sin and evil. Forgiveness acknowledges that a terrible wrong has been done and seeks to do something about it. God desires to forgive. "The Lord is compassionate and gracious, slow to anger and abounding in love. He will not always accuse, nor will he harbor his anger forever. He does not treat us as our sins deserve or repay according to our iniquities. For as high as the heavens are above the earth, so great is his love for those who fear him. As far as the east is from the west, so far has he removed our transgressions from us" (Psalm 103:8-12, NIV).
>
> Jesus makes forgiveness possible. Isn't it amazing that, even with something as terrible as murder, God is available and willing to forgive you? If my God is willing, how could I not be?

Nick's response, which arrived within a few weeks, infuriated me. He demanded money to purchase a TV before he would speak to me. I wrote him back and told him this wasn't a "you scratch my back and I'll scratch yours" relationship. I said that the God of the universe loves him so much that a stranger in California would write him, and that he needed to get on his knees and thank God for this letter because God's love and forgiveness was the only reason he was getting it.

My whole purpose of writing to Nick was to let him know that I wanted to come to meet him and share the Gospel with him out of obedience to God. But we exchanged several letters before he would even place me on his visitor list.

Around the same time, I was writing Nick and trying to arrange a meeting, I could feel God pulling me in a new direction. On the one hand, I was scared to leave my job; it was all I had known since I was 17 years old. However, I was ready for a change. After talking with Kevin about the possibility of making a change, he suggested that I create a list of the pros and cons of leaving, and that we discuss what God revealed. I ended up with a full page of pros and only one con: money. I presented the list to Kevin and, after discussing it, he said I should take the leap.

Things moved rapidly after that. I called John, the owner of the company where I worked, and scheduled an appointment in our Anaheim office. I told him I had some things I needed to discuss with him and that it was imperative that we meet in person ASAP. By the nature of my request, he knew it was important. The day before I was scheduled to meet with John, I gathered the employees who worked in my chain of command together in the training room. I told them I was going to the corporate office the next morning to submit my resignation and wanted to let them know first, in case— due to corporate policy governing departing employees—I didn't come back. I shared how grateful I was for them and for how, over the years, we had grown to be like a family. I told them how proud I was of all they'd done for the company and the community, and then I closed by praying over them, shocking some, I'm sure.

On the day of my appointment with John, he was prepared to discuss the company's financial statements with me. I intervened, saying he needed to hear what I had to say before he talked. He kept telling me he wanted to review the financials first, but I held firm. "John, I need to tell you what I came here to discuss," I said. "I'm giving my resignation and will be leaving the company in 30 days." Stunned, he looked at me and said, "Deborah, you cannot leave in 30 days." I said, "Yes, I'm leaving; my last day will be May 31."

After 34 years in the security industry, I left to do ministry full-time. It was a new dawn and a new day. I believed everything was coming together and that I was stepping into my destiny. This was an incredible time for me. Walking out the door at Kern Security, I told Nikki, my assistant, "Don't worry, I'm hooking up with The Great Adventurer!" I had no idea just how wild the adventure would be.

To celebrate the end of my security-industry career and spend time with my kids, we left on an East Coast vacation. In New York, I took the kids to Times Square and to see "Spiderman" on Broadway. Next, we drove the back roads to Niagara Falls; Canada; Michigan; Lancaster, Pennsylvania; and Philadelphia. We saw the Liberty Bell, Williamsburg, Washington, D.C., Jamestown, and toured all over the East Coast. In Virginia, we met up with my brother, Steven, and my old friend, Reggie, who accompanied me to visit places from my childhood. I was trying to fill in the blanks. I wanted to know the truth so the truth could set me free.[5]

---

[5] John 8:32

Chapter 19

Never Give Up

*"Therefore, strengthen your feeble arms and your weak knees.
'Make level paths for your feet,' so that the lame may
not be disabled, but rather healed."*
— Hebrews 12:12-13

Starting and running a nonprofit was completely different from any experience I'd had in my business career. I needed to raise my own financial support, recruit volunteers, and raise awareness for the cause. I was fortunate to work with leaders from Samaritan's Purse, Kids Around the World, and International Christian Ministry, and learn what it really meant to trust God in *all* situations. I thought I'd trusted Him before; however, it became clear that I had a lot to learn.

Kevin and I had been married in 1993 and, as our twentieth wedding anniversary approached, I began dreaming about renewing our vows in Yosemite Valley, something I'd always wanted to do. With its giant Sequoias, magnificent tunnel views, and breathtaking waterfalls, this part of California is my favorite place in the world.

Little did I know that Kevin had secretly planned a trip to Yosemite for our anniversary.

With our anniversary fast approaching, I received an unexpected phone call from Daughters of Destiny, a Florida-based ministry that invited me to speak at a prison in Madison, Indiana. With Levi's sixteenth birthday and our wedding anniversary both coming up, though, a trip to Indiana would mean I would miss one or both of these major events. Feeling conflicted, I studied a map of Indiana, noting that the Madison prison and Nick Harbison's prison were only a few hours apart. The trip would provide a chance to finally visit Nick and speak in a prison outside of California. I was excited. It felt like God was opening the door for me to meet Nick at long last.

I shared with Kevin why I felt like the trip was divinely orchestrated, how God seemed to be opening the door for me, and how the travel was feasible. After praying about it, Kevin said he thought I should go. That's when he also told me about the surprise arrangements he'd made for us to spend our anniversary in Yosemite. Now I was more torn than ever. I told him I wasn't going on the trip; there was no way I wanted to miss our anniversary celebration. But Kevin told me he believed I really needed to go, adding that he would take care of canceling everything. I somewhat reluctantly agreed with him and booked my travel for five days in Pendleton, Indiana.

After all my plans were in place, I received a letter from Nick saying that he wasn't ready to meet. I emailed back, telling him I was still coming. And I did. First, I visited my nephew, Chris, in Ohio, then rented a car and drove to Pendleton, where Nick was incarcerated in a maximum-security unit of the Pendleton Correctional Facility. When I checked into my hotel, I met a very sweet lady named Becky, who served the continental breakfast each morning. In casual conversation, she asked me what had brought me to Indiana. I explained I'd flown in to visit the man who'd murdered my niece—the man known nationwide as the Cornfield Killer. Shocked by my disclosure, Becky said she remembered hearing about the horrible crime at the time it happened and asked me to tell her more. I saw Becky every day before and after going to the prison and got to know her well.

~

***...A friend told me later, "God loves you so much,
He closed Yosemite just for you."***

~

The day I went to prison to see Nick was intense. Providing my identity to the front-counter staff and saying I was there to visit Nick Harbison felt awkward. Afterward, I took a seat and waited. The phone inside the secured area had a large bell on top of it and, each time it rang, I could feel my chest tighten in anticipation of being called back. Forty-five minutes later, they called my name. As I approached the counter, wondering what I would say to Nick, the correctional officer told me I couldn't see the man I'd traveled 2,000 miles to visit. "He doesn't want to come down for any visitors today," the officer explained.

I went back to my hotel room and emailed Nick.

I am sitting here in my hotel room wondering why I'm here in Pendleton, Indiana. I have to say I was a little frustrated when you denied visiting me. Tomorrow is my twentieth wedding anniversary and I'm here and not home, trying to see a man who will not visit with me. How CRAZY is that?

I knew that there was a possibility that you wouldn't visit me, but I thought you would come. So, when the officer came and told me that you didn't want to have a visit, it was disheartening. I have asked Chaplain Dodd to see you and, hopefully, he will do that tomorrow. I'm going to try and visit again tomorrow. Nick, what are you so afraid of? Have you thought about that? Why are you allowing the Enemy to continue to use you? Haven't you given him enough of your life? For some reason, you look at this meeting as dreadful and I look at it as amazing. Amazing that God would change my heart so much toward you. Most people would never reach out and continue to reach out even when rejected.

Nick, you're not just rejecting me, you are rejecting who I represent. I am Rebekah's aunt. That means you come face-to-face with your sin. Do you think it's easy being on the other end of this? I was nervous and sick to my stomach. I have anticipated this for a while; but I was also so excited because, Nick, the very hard thing for you to understand is how much God loves Nicholas Harbison. It's absolutely amazing! I know because I'm here, because of His directing.

I don't know when you will receive this email, but I hope you seek God's direction about visiting with me and stop listening to the voice of the Enemy. How bad can it be visiting with me? You might be pleasantly surprised at how good the visit can be. I hope you have a wonderful day.

I got up early the next day to be at the prison by 9 a.m. but, again, Nick wouldn't see me. Returning to the hotel around 9:45, I entered the lobby only to see on the big-screen TV a news story about … Yosemite. I was instantly bummed. That's exactly where I wanted to be right this minute for my anniversary, not in Indiana by myself. As I listened to the newscast, however, a shocking storyline unfolded. Yosemite National Park was closed due to a government shutdown! Had I not canceled my trip, I still wouldn't have been able to go there. In that moment, God showed me that, instead of missing out on something wonderful, He'd divinely arranged every detail. As a friend told me later, "God loves you so much, He closed Yosemite just for you."

The next morning, I went through the same visitor routine at the prison as the day before, eager to share the Gospel with Nick. And, just like the day before, Nick again refused to see me. It just didn't make sense. I knew that God had led me to Pendleton and opened doors for me all along the way. Nick's refusal to see me didn't add up. I was angry with God and wondered why He was toying with me. I was ready to throw in the towel—not only on seeing Nick but on pursuing a ministry with Be Finally Free. *Why was I wasting my time?* I thought.

After spending five days trying to see the murderer who'd killed one of my family members, I headed to Madison to speak at the prison for Daughters of Destiny. I was completely drained. I had no energy to deliver a message to anyone. What was I going to give to these ladies? When I spoke, I shared what happened with Nick and how drained I was. As I was sharing my story with the inmates, I noticed a correctional officer who'd stopped to listen to what I was saying. I asked the inmates to stand up if they needed prayer for forgiveness. Then I called them forward and said it's not just about standing up; it's about stepping forward to commit that you *will* forgive those who've harmed you. When I looked up from the prayer, a correctional officer was standing in front of me to commit to forgiveness.

I spent a few days in Madison before returning to California. When I got home, I wrote Nick, telling him I didn't know if we would ever officially meet, encouraging him, and assuring him that God wanted to have a relationship with him. I said that God was relentless and cares. I couldn't understand it, but I knew God wanted Nick to know.

After I returned home to California, I received a letter from Becky, the hotel worker I'd befriended. It read:

Dear Debbie,

Just wanted to say hi and thank you for ministering to me while you were at the Fairfield. You will never know how much you helped me. I really needed to hear some encouraging words. I have so much more to say but my life is hectic right now. I'll write again soon. I think of you often and I am amazed how God used you to touch my broken heart. You are so special to me.

Thank you!
Becky

I immediately replied and, soon afterward, received another letter:

Hey Debbie,

It was wonderful to have you respond so quickly. If someone would have called me from the hotel and told me you were there Monday morning, I would have come running. It would have been great to see you again and chat for a while.

I'm so sorry that Nicholas didn't come down to see you. I'm inspired by how many times you tried ... kind of like that relentless God I've been reading about in *Crazy Love* [a book I'd read and given her]. That book is just what I needed and, every time I read it, I think of you and how I KNOW that God placed you there to minister to me. I was just about on the verge of collapse from all of the stress from my daughter and what she goes through each day. I would put a smile on my face and try so hard not to let anyone see the pain I was feeling. It was an effort just to go to work each day.

Wednesday was my last day at work and that was wonderful. I needed to let go of that job and relieve some of the stress. They gave me a beautiful going-away party yesterday ... I felt so special. LOL.

How did your ministry to the women go in southern Indiana? I hope it went well and that God continues to use you in miraculous ways. I'm honored that He allowed our paths to cross. I somehow believe that, if we lived close to each other, we would be close friends. You have such a beautiful spirit and so many gifts that God is using. I will continue to pray for Nicholas, that he will find God's love and forgiveness ... and I'll continue to pray for you, that God will continue the work He has begun in you ... and the ones who are fortunate enough to meet you.

Stay in touch when you have time.

Love and prayers,
Becky

During my trip to Indiana, at times I felt as though I was drowning. To stay afloat, I focused on God's Word. Letters of encouragement I received from a group of supporters were also a great help. After reading Becky's letter, I began to realize the trip was more impactful than I could have ever imagined. God had used me to plant seeds of love and radical obedience to Him. The prison's correctional officers, Becky, and all who were following my trip and encouraging me along the way—each one heard and saw His work through me, underscoring that God is the author of love and forgiveness. While I'd originally thought that going to Pendleton was about Nick and me, I later learned that God was using the story of my "journey of obedience" to change lives in prisons, churches, and elsewhere, all over the world. By saying "yes" to God's will and "no" to my own, people were learning how to forgive. And, as if that weren't enough blessing and satisfaction, God made sure Yosemite was closed just for me!

Chapter 20

Liberia, March 2014

"Make a dent where you're sent."
— Unknown

Since the beginning of my faith journey, I deeply desired to know the truth about myself, about God, and my purpose. My first trip to Liberia helped me learn that obedience is the initial step toward understanding truth. During that trip, God required me to be honest and authentic about my own life by forcing me to open up and share my story in public.

Jesus told those who had faith in Him, "If you keep on obeying what I have said, you truly are my disciples and you will know the truth and the truth will set you free" (John 8:31-32, CEV). I wanted to be free. Free from spiritual and emotional bondage. Free from being on the fence about God, who He is, and His unconditional love for me. Free from the shame of my past. Free to walk in the life God had for me.

Amazingly, I was excited to return to Liberia, even though

I told myself I'd never go back again. I knew I needed to return to the place where God had begun a miraculous transformation in my life. A place where being uncomfortable, miserable, scared, and surrendered enabled me to hear God and allow Him to speak through me, if only for 15 minutes.

~

I had been transformed from a scared, timid, closed-off hermit to an outgoing, sold-out, on-fire, full-of-life Jesus Freak boldly praying for a rugged rebel warlord.

~

On that first trip, I was so hard-headed. This time, God had my full attention and I was all ears. I wanted everyone to see how amazing God was. I wanted to show how bold I was in Him, and how determined I was to obey Him, no matter the cost. This was my chance to share with everyone how God used that first speaking engagement to change everything in my life.

I expressed to Kevin my desire to return to Liberia. Unbeknownst to me, Kevin, too, wanted to go back. In fact, he'd received a $1,300 bonus for his twentieth anniversary at work and already was thinking about using the money for the trip. I didn't know about his desires and plans until I opened a Christmas card from him on Christmas morning. The message in the card read:

> I have been wanting to go back to Liberia. I would love to see all the friends I have made over the years, maybe one last time. I don't know what it is about that country that makes me want to go back. I decided I would look at the cost to fly to Africa and it was exactly the amount I had. I came up with a great idea that I should probably talk to you about going before buying the ticket!!! One morning

I was having my quiet time and the thought of Haiti or Africa came to mind and I said I NEED to go in early 2014. I looked again at the flight to Liberia and it was still exactly the amount I had so I said 'That's it; I'm going to see my friends.'

Then I remember you telling me about Pastor Browne calling you. I know there is no way we can both go. I don't want to leave Hope and Levi with someone that long and we can't afford for both of us to go. As I sat and thought about getting to go, it was like a voice saying 'Let Debbie go instead.' I knew this wasn't from God, so I let it go. A few days later, when the same thing happened, I wanted to argue with God and tell Him why I needed to go. This was my money, right? I worked 20 years to get it. That's when I realized it's God's money—our money—and I'm often just being selfish.

I wrote Daniel McGee and Pastor Morris Browne, Sr. to see what they thought, and they said it would be GREAT to see you there. So, with joy that you will be going, but really bummed I won't, I bought you the ticket to fly to my beloved Liberia.

I love you,
Kevin

I was so excited! Kevin had sacrificed greatly to give his ticket to me, and I immediately shared with my friends and family on Facebook how I felt about this beautiful gesture of love:

This Christmas was so special! I was able to watch and

listen to my husband preach at MTCC [Mountain Top Community Church] on Christmas Eve, then we came home to a fun-filled Christmas Eve night with our family. Chinese food, gifts, and a crazy white elephant game. It was amazing, but none of it prepared me for Christmas morning. After opening all our gifts, Kevin gave me a card with a letter so beautifully written that, as I read it to my family, Kevin and I were both in tears. Kevin has been saving his money from his twentieth anniversary at Kern Security, plus other money, to go on a mission trip back to Haiti or, maybe, to Liberia. Kevin has been to Liberia eight times and I know how badly he wants to return. Unbelievably, I have wanted to go back to Liberia for years, too, but I was sure it would be Kevin and me going together. I'm so excited that God is allowing me the opportunity to go back to Liberia to share how the trip in 2008 opened the door to Be Finally Free, Inc. I love you, Kevin Ormonde; I know what a sacrifice this really is. Thank you for loving me enough to completely give up everything for me.

Within two hours after posting on social media, an anonymous ticket was gifted for Kevin to go with me. He got the same exact flight as mine. To this day, I don't know who the gift-giver was. After receiving the ticket, I posted this on Facebook:

I just received a Christmas Miracle—Kevin is going to Liberia with me! Some very special person spoke with Lisa and told her that they wanted to purchase Kevin's airplane ticket so he could go on the trip.
How do you thank someone who blesses you beyond

belief? Thank you to the special person who allowed God to use you to bless us. I'm so excited that we are going to do this trip together. I can't wait to see how God is going to work as we travel to Africa.

When we arrived in Africa, it was fantastic! We did several radio shows, went to four prisons, spoke at a marriage conference, and I spoke at a women's conference. We got to attend a court hearing to see how a Liberian trial was conducted. We spoke at a security conference where Kevin also received an award for his friendship with an international missions organization called ELWA (Eternal Love Winning Africa), and we both spoke in different churches.

But the most amazing part of the whole trip was when I was asked to meet with a man who had been a Liberian rebel general during the nation's civil war. (Fortunately for me, they didn't tell me that's who he was before I met him!) Everywhere we visited was full of life, vibrant colors, dancing, and excitement. I had been transformed from a scared, timid, closed-off hermit to an outgoing, sold-out, on-fire, full-of-life Jesus Freak boldly praying for a rugged rebel warlord.

I was learning what it really meant to know the truth and be set free. I'd wanted to have an authentic relationship with Jesus, but it wasn't until I decided to be radically obedient to Him that I felt free. Freedom meant re-learning everything I'd ever thought I knew about God, religion, and living a bondage-free life. God liberated me to walk in a relationship with Him and be the woman he created me to be. I learned that being set free wasn't about doing what I wanted to do; it was about exercising the God-given freedom to do what I *ought* to do. I realized that God wasn't giving me rules; He was allowing me to see that I had the free will to choose—be it right or wrong. Freedom is the ability to obey God and choose His will for my life, not out of obligation, but out of love for Him. And I was finally experiencing true freedom within. "If the son sets you free, you will be free indeed" (John 8:36, ESV).

Chapter 21

Unveiling the Truth

"For everything there is a season,
and a time for every matter under heaven."
— Ecclesiastes 3:1 (ESV)

I was spending around 80 hours a week on the ministry, attending to every detail. It was God and me. Be Finally Free's first annual fundraising gala was held at Olive Knolls church in September 2014. It took a lot of effort to pull the event together on my own—from designing the marketing materials, planning the order of events, securing silent-auction items, and raising the funds. Three hundred people attended.

That evening, Nikki, my assistant from Kern Security, was helping with the silent auction. I remember looking over at her and thinking, *I need a Nikki*. But I also knew there was no way we could afford to hire her. I knew what she needed to earn, and we didn't have the funds. I dismissed the idea and focused on the event, which turned out to be a great success.

Shortly after the gala, I was asked to speak again for Daughters of Destiny in Madison, Indiana. I immediately recognized that this would present another opportunity for me to try to see Nick. So, I flew to Ohio again and, after spending time with family, drove to Pendleton, planning to be there only one day.

~

He opened my eyes to see Nick in His image and blinded my eyes to judgment.

~

The next morning, I met Becky for breakfast. It was so nice to catch up with her and discover what God was doing in her life. I knew that, if Nick refused to meet with me again, I would at least have had the chance to visit with Becky.

After my breakfast with Becky, I headed to the prison. To my own amazement, I found myself, once again, walking toward that big, dreary, brown rectangular building, hoping Nick would finally meet with me. I signed in at the security desk and the same dark-haired officer was there. "You're back again?" he asked. I was surprised he remembered me.

I went to the ever-familiar waiting area and paced the floor. My stomach was in knots. I was hoping so desperately that Nick would see me this time. Then the phone rang and the intercom announced, "Visitor for Harbison!" My knees were shaking as I walked through the cold steel gate separating me from the visitor's room.

I saw him sitting at a small, square, grey table, staring straight at me. He looked just like that same cold-blooded killer I'd seen on "America's Most Wanted." I sat down across from him and looked into his eyes. I couldn't believe what I was seeing! The moment I looked into his eyes, my perception shifted. I saw a man made in God's image, not a cold-blooded killer. He didn't change, but God was changing the way I saw him.

After a moment of silence, I said, "Nick, do you know how much God loves you? He loves you so much I can't even have a bean-and-cheese burrito without God hassling me!"

"I'd give anything for a bean-and-cheese burrito right now," Nick responded.

I laughed. God used a bean-and-cheese burrito to break the ice between me and my niece's murderer.

I shared the Gospel with Nick. I told him that God doesn't see him as the murderer and me as Debbie the evangelist. He sees us equally. No favorites. Nick didn't talk too much; he just listened, not seeming to understand much of what I was saying. And, then, before I knew it, our time was up. I prayed with him and left the prison, almost skipping more than walking. Not because I'd seen Nick, but because I thought this chapter in my life was finally closed.

I got in my car and headed toward Madison. On the way, God put it on my heart to find a church for Nick. I stopped at the first church I saw, shared Nick's story, explained how he needed a church, and pointed out that they were right next door to the prison. They volunteered to connect me with a woman who was trying to start a prison ministry at Pendleton. An hour later, we had lunch and, as I shared my story of forgiveness and of God's relentless love, she was flabbergasted. I told her that God put it on my heart that Nick needed a mentor and a support system to help him focus on a relationship with God and reconciliation to others. She readily agreed to help.

Back on the road to Madison, where I had several speaking engagements planned, I was still processing what it meant to see a man in God's own image. I'd never before experienced an instant heart change like that. Later, as I shared the experience with a friend, she said, "God blinded you that day." It's true: He opened my eyes to see Nick in His image and blinded my eyes to judgment.

While still in Indiana, I got a call from my brother, Steven, that Nancy, Rebekah's mother and Steven's ex-wife, had passed away. I was torn between attending the funeral and visiting Steven so I could tell him about Nick. Sensing it was the right time to bring Steven up to speed on all God had been doing with Nick, I flew to Virginia. As I prepared my heart to talk to Steven, Reggie and I spent time re-visiting our childhood neighborhood. We drove by our family's house, just down the street from Reggie's. As I was photographing the exterior, the owners invited me to come inside. To my surprise, it looked exactly the same as when I'd lived there over 40 years earlier.

As children, Reggie and I used to always spend time in a cemetery, and we decided to stop by. Over the years, I'd dreamed countless times of a white concrete tree. When we arrived at the cemetery, one of the first things I saw was the actual white tombstone that was symbolized by a tree in my recurring dreams. I was amazed how, in my dreams, God had planted a beautiful, symbol of life in the center of a place of death.

After visiting the cemetery, we drove to the old town plaza, blasting Elton John as we sang out of the open windows with everyone staring at us as we passed by. Lost in the moment, we looped the streets and the same song three times. Then we left to see my brother.

On the way to Steven's home, I prayed that God would give me the right words and prepare his heart. That night, Reggie and I went to dinner with Steven and his wife, Thia. The next day, Reggie and I returned to Steven's house and Reggie stayed with Thia while Steven and I went for a drive. I didn't know what to say or how to broach the topic of Nick. Praying silently for words, we drove down by the beach and parked. Then, I pulled out of my tote bag a book with Rebekah's picture on the cover. The book contained all of my letters to and from Nick. As soon as he saw the book, Steven started crying. I expected him to yell at me. I thought he would ask how I could have anything to do with the murderer of his daughter. I believed he would wonder what kind of sister would betray him. However, I was shocked to hear what came out of his mouth: "Does he know Jesus as his Lord and Savior?" Right then, I knew I didn't have to tell my brother the details. God showed me how perfect His timing was. He had gone before me and prepared Steven's heart.

> For everything there is a season, and a time for every matter under heaven:
> a time to be born, and a time to die;
> a time to plant, and a time to pluck up what is planted;
> a time to kill, and a time to heal;
> a time to break down, and a time to build up;
> a time to weep, and a time to laugh;
> a time to mourn, and a time to dance;
> a time to cast away stones, and a time to gather stones together;
> a time to embrace, and a time to refrain from embracing;
> a time to seek, and a time to lose;
> a time to keep, and a time to cast away;
> a time to tear, and a time to sew;
> a time to keep silence, and a time to speak;
> a time to love, and a time to hate;
> a time for war, and a time for peace.
>
> (Ecclesiastes 3:1-8, ESV)

Chapter 22

Freeing the Prisoner
From Within

"So, Jesus said to those who believed in him, 'If you obey my teaching,
you are really my disciples; you will know the truth,
and the truth will set you free.'"
— John 8:31-32 (GNT)

From the moment I boarded that white church bus as a little girl, filled with anticipation of being awarded my prized blue leather Bible with my name engraved on the cover, I lived a life filled with chaos, danger, and disappointment. Running away—indulging myself with everything the world had to offer in the vain attempt to fill a void that only God could fill— seemed to be the easiest escape. I was in search of something more than religion and I heard it could be found in a relationship with Jesus. But it didn't make sense.

My hunger for connection was insatiable. I looked for love in relationships with men, with my family, and in the church. I sought satisfaction through climbing the corporate ladder. But I could never find the peace and fulfillment I craved through relationships, religion, or work. I found it only in my relationship with Jesus.

Freeing the Prisoner from Within started with me hearing the Word of God. But He wanted more than a hearer of the Word. He wanted a doer.[6] He wanted obedience over sacrifice, and forgiveness over hatred.[7] Obedience meant I needed to surrender my will to God's will.

I knew what it meant to be a good leader, but I didn't know how to follow, or even what following entailed. Sure, I'd always wanted the people I managed to follow me. What I really wanted, though, was for them simply to do what I said. Based on my misguided notions about leading and following, I'd thought God was the same way: He just wanted me to be under his thumb. But that was not the radical obedience Jesus asked of His followers.

I was taught that "surrender" and "obedience" were bad words … nasty words. They meant being under someone else's control. I was taught to push through, not to wave the white flag. Never give up or give in. Press for more. But God says the opposite: I could never free the prisoner within if I didn't surrender to Him. God says that, when I am weak, He is strong.

My life's circumstances have increased my faith and made me stronger by trusting God in the midst of everything. So often, God gave me peace that surpassed all understanding. I learned to take pleasure in hardships and persecutions by staying focused and allowing God to be my Comforter, assured that, through these hardships and persecution, God was deepening my relationship with Him. This type of trust in a loving God who has my best interest at

---

[6] James 1:22
[7] 1 Samuel 15:22, Ephesians 4:31-32

heart is what true surrender looks like. What a contradiction to the brawler mentality I was taught on the streets.

One time, when I was speaking in prison, God helped me see what surrender really looks like. I was in a large facility with around 200 prisoners in the room. A guard looked on while I was speaking on a topic of surrender. I noticed the guard had a big ring of keys and I asked to borrow them. He handed them over willingly, not knowing what I was going to do. As I held up each key, I named something God calls us to surrender in order to be free. One is your children. One is religion. One is your relationships. One is your career. One is your drugs, and on and on. I said God wants you to surrender all of these areas. I then took the keys and threw them to the prisoners.

~

You can't have your will and God's will and call it surrender.
God doesn't work that way. He doesn't bless duality.

~

The guard, meanwhile, looked shocked that I'd given his keys to the inmates. And that's when I realized what real surrender looks like. The look of fear on the guard's face instantly revealed how the Enemy, Satan, feels when we truly surrender our life to God. Obedience involves an act of our will, regardless of our feelings. According to Wikipedia, "surrender in spirituality and religion means that a believer completely gives up his own will and subjects his thoughts, ideas, and deeds to the will and teachings of a higher power."[8]

Billy Graham, the late evangelist, once said, "If you want change in your life, if you want forgiveness and peace and joy that you've never known before, God demands total surrender. He becomes

---

[8] Surrender (religion), *Wikipedia*, Wikimedia Foundation, last modified on May 5, 2021, https://en.wikipedia.org/wiki/Surrender_(religion)#:~:text=To%20surrender%20in%20spirituality%20and,dominating%20force%20and%20their%20will, accessed May 6, 2021.

the Lord and ruler of your life." You can't have your will and God's will and call it surrender. God doesn't work that way. He doesn't bless duality. When you surrender, there is no compromise. It's all in or nothing. To free the prisoner from within, you must surrender your will to the will of God. "So, if the Son sets you free, you will be free indeed" (John 8:36, ESV).

If you've been living as a chameleon, riding the rollercoaster of life and unable to get off, or if you've never been able to experience the power of God in your life, today is the day. Decide now to surrender your life to God. Will it be hard? Yes! Will you experience difficulties? Yes! Will the world have many injustices? Yes! We were never promised a smooth, comfortable journey. However, God says:

> Consider it pure joy, my brothers and sisters, whenever you face trials of many kinds, because you know that the testing of your faith produces perseverance. Let perseverance finish its work so that you may be mature and complete, not lacking anything. If any of you lacks wisdom, you should ask God, who gives generously to all without finding fault, and it will be given to you. But when you ask, you must believe and not doubt, because the one who doubts is like a wave of the sea, blown and tossed by the wind. That person should not expect to receive anything from the Lord. Such a person is double-minded and unstable in all they do (James 1:2-8, NIV).

God is standing with arms wide open waiting for YOU to say "Yes!" When you do, buckle your seatbelt and get ready for an adventure of a lifetime. Get ready to be finally free!

A Letter From the Executive Director
of Be Finally Free, Inc.

I first met Debbie in 1994 when she hired my father for a sales position with Kern Security. Not long afterward, I became a sitter for Levi and Hope, Debbie and Kevin's two youngest children. I then accepted a filing clerk position at Kern, eventually working my way up to the position of Debbie's assistant.

I have witnessed Debbie's consistent compassion toward individuals and our community, and how she has invested countless hours and resources through numerous outreach programs. I've watched her joyfully develop her own nonprofit—and many others, as well—with a vision to better the community.

Her passion and love for people and her experience serving as a board member for several nonprofits opened her heart and mind to establish Be Finally Free, Inc. (BFF) in Bakersfield in 2008. Three years later, when Debbie left Kern Security, I asked—with tears of anticipation and fear in my eyes—if she knew what she was getting herself into. "Don't worry," she responded. "I'm hooking up with The Great Adventurer!" I had no idea that this adventure was going to be mine, too. Taking a month away from all work to focus on her relationship with God underscored how committed Debbie was to ensuring her calling.

I continued working for Kern Security while Debbie spent time with God, traveled with her family, and visited many churches and ministries, where she built collaborative relationships to further the vision God had given her. During this time, I was also pursuing my Christian walk while serving in children's ministry, leading a praise team, and taking on a strong leadership role directly under the Children's Pastor of my church.

~

Our connections weren't going to come through and give us the glory. This was going to be about God and His will for His glory.

~

Debbie is such a large part of my life and has always been a big motivator for me to step into all that God has created me to be. This new chapter became a period where growing my relationship with God became my priority. I was encouraged, nervous, and scared all at the same time. Debbie's transition to full-time ministry stirred my curiosity and we kept in touch over the next few years. But I wasn't ready to join her team just yet. I needed time to grow in ways that, ultimately, would be necessary to help Debbie and BFF flourish.

In November of 2014, after helping with BFF's silent auction during the ministry's first fundraising gala, Debbie texted, inviting me to lunch. Instantly, I knew something was up. Whenever Debbie asked to meet me in person, I knew she had something big going on and I could hardly wait to hear about her next big project. Her next text read, "I want to talk about you leaving Kern Security and coming on board with BFF." She had no way to know that, just two days earlier, I'd told my husband that I was feeling pulled away from Kern and longing for a life change.

During lunch the next day, Debbie said she wanted and needed me to come on board with BFF. She advised me up-front that she only had enough money to pay me for three months and that I couldn't make my decision based on my love for her—it had to be what God was calling me to do. She suggested I talk to my husband and pray about it before giving her an answer. (Little did she know,

I already had my confirmation, but I was scared to take this next step.) The next day, I told Debbie I was all in. After giving Kern my two-week's notice and taking time off for the Christmas holidays, we started fresh in the new year, working out of Debbie's home.

Two-thousand-fifteen was a year of massive transition for me. I lost my brother to an alcohol addiction and I consistently questioned my qualifications to serve in a ministry that focused on helping people with addictions. But Debbie, as she'd done so many times before, continued to encourage me and remind me of God's promises.

After four months, we moved our offices from Debbie's home to a shared office with the founder of Wellspring Personal Development, Sherry Rose. Sherry was on BFF's board and both of our ministries were in the early developmental stages and needed office space. We set up shop and took pictures for all of our family and supporters to see. We were so excited to have bricks-and-mortar to serve as the foundation for BFF's future growth.

Debbie and I started planning events and booking speaking engagements to get the word out about the ministry. We set appointments, met people in the community, and I took on the administrative duties for all the different programs we were running. As Debbie began visiting area churches to get the word out, she quickly learned that churches can tend to compete with each other for dollars and members. So, Debbie pivoted and tapped her business contacts to help spread the word. Although they said they loved what we were doing, we found it was difficult to obtain much-needed financial support and resources. We were exhausted and began to learn that BFF's growth wasn't about us. Our connections weren't going to come through and give us the glory. This was going to be about God and His will for His glory.

Initially, the ministry focused on pen pal letters to teens in the juvenile system, with no idea of how the vision would continue to expand. Through the many avenues and directions taken over the years, BFF has evolved into a ministry with the following vision and mission:

The Vision of Be Finally Free, Inc. is to be a community overcoming the effects of crime, poverty, and hardships through the love of Jesus Christ. Our Mission is to restore and equip those impacted by addiction, crime, incarceration, and poverty by providing education, instilling life skills, and giving hope to overcome their circumstances.

Over the last several years, BFF has developed programs to help disciple, educate, and build relationships with our constituents. These programs are offered through a curriculum designed by BFF and certified through the Kern County Department of Human Services and Probation. Additionally, BFF orchestrates several community outreaches and classes throughout the year and provides ongoing counseling services through many channels.

Be Finally Free is fully funded and financially supported by private donations. Between 2017 and 2020, BFF has helped over 24,727 program participants and invested over 141,805 community hours.

At BFF, we know that our most important goal is to help people know Jesus intimately. It is through that relationship that they will become transformed, freeing the prisoner from within.

If you would like to join Be Finally Free on our journey toward "redeeming the lost, to send to the lost," please contact us:

Nichole Linenberger
Executive Director
Be Finally Free, Inc.
Info@befinallyfree.org
(661) 489-5952
befinallyfree.org
501c3 Tax Id # 27-2564485

Upcoming Book

A New Beginning

November 2015

Debbie,

It's Sunday morning and I just got done watching Joel, a powerful speaker on TV. I've tried to watch other preachers on TV, but none of them have been able to hold my attention. But, believe it or not, I actually look forward to watching him each week. Today, as I was watching him, I started thinking about you. Yeah, he's a good speaker and storyteller, but if it wasn't for you, I wouldn't be watching him or reading the Bible. You refused to give up on me and showed me nothing but kindness even after everything I have put you and your family through. To be honest with you, I am envious of your faith. I want that kind of faith someday. You have made me want to be a better person.

Thank you, Debbie, for everything you do for me. I am so very grateful.

Nick

Acknowledgements

There are so many people to thank for their help with this book. I would have never had the experiences that fill so many of these pages had it not been for my Mom, Dad, and brother, Steven. We were not the average family; however, we have loyalty to one another and a love that most will never understand.

Kevin, thank you for loving me, especially when I'm unlovable. This book would not have been possible without you. You have allowed me to be me, to chase my dreams. We both know what a sacrifice this has been. I love you to the stars, the moon, and to China and back again.

Lisa, Amy, Joshua, Devin, Levi, and Hope: our life has been an adventure. I have loved every moment of it. Thank you for teaching me that my past does not dictate my future. You are my legacy and I thank God for you every day.

My very own BFF, Reggie. Thank you for driving me all over Virginia so I could remember all the details to write this book. It still boggles the mind how we stayed connected all those years when I was on the run—and we didn't even have the internet! Mrs. Smith would have NEVER believed we would stay friends for over 50 years.

Nikki, thank you for going on this journey with me. There are days when we are so excited because of all that we can see God doing. Then, there are days we want to beat our heads against the wall because of the pain we feel as we watch somebody we love fall back into the mire. Be Finally Free, Inc. is what it is because of you. I love doing life with you.

Vanessa, day in and day out, you have been an integral part of Be Finally Free, Inc. Thank you for proofreading and listening, and for your insight, which helped get this book to print.

To My Lord and Savior, Jesus, I could absolutely do NOTHING without you. Thank you for loving me exactly where I am and for never, ever, giving up on me. You have been my role model and taught me what it means to be a servant to the least of these.

Madison Porter, thank you for designing and drawing the map to help readers follow my crazy journey. You were such a joy to work with, you took all the ideas and made them work. I appreciate you so much.

Elizabeth Cunningham, my editor, where do I begin? Without a doubt, God placed you in my life to take this book to the next level. We bonded immediately and our connection was so inspirational. Thank you just doesn't seem enough for all your hard work and dedication to this book and to me.

Lauren Patterson, without you this book would not exist. I spent over six years on chapter one! I had an outline and a ton of ideas. Then, one day, I asked if you would help me get this book out of my head and onto paper. Being overwhelmed in your own life you still said "yes." For almost a year, we sat in the beautiful fireside room where I would tell you my story. Some days, we were both in tears; other days, we laughed so hard. We had many counseling sessions as we worked our way through over 40 years of chaos. Our weekend trips to the ranch to disconnect and get away from the distractions were incredible. I will always be grateful to you for making this book a reality. We have both learned so much about writing, love, forgiveness, mercy, and God's destiny for our lives. Thank you from the bottom of my heart.

Chesterfield Mother, 39, Convicted

A 39-year-old woman has been convicted in Chesterfield County Court of contributing to the delinquency of a minor and handed a ~~six-month suspended jail~~ sentence.

Mrs. Vella Marie Acorn, of the 2900 block Galena Ave., was convicted May 17. She pleaded guilty to the charge after it was lowered from a charge of secreting her 12-year-old daughter out of the state. The daughter had been committed to the care of the state Department of Welfare and Institutions.

Immediately after her conviction last Thursday, Mrs. Acorn was arrested again by Chesterfield police and charged with defrauding the Chesterfield-Colonial Heights Department of Social Services by failing to report income from a job.

She is free on $300 bond pending a June 1 County Court hearing.

...T OF VIOLENCE
Bombings, Fights Erupt in Lynwood

Lynwood police today believe they have linked a night of violence that included gang fights, a chain beating and two firebombings.

A 19-year-old Lynwood youth, Lawrence Bell, was injured in one of the fights, which occurred shortly before 9 p.m. and was taken to St. Francis Hospital.

Police, summoned to 10724 San Jose Ave., said Bell told them he had been in front of the residence when two vans and a car pulled up to the curb, with several Latin males getting out and striking him with tire irons. Police said Bell was also stabbed in the back twice.

About 45 minutes earlier, police had responded to a report of a large fight in the 10700 block of Osgood Avenue, which parallels San Jose and is one block east of San Jose.

Officers broke up that fight, no complaint was desired, and "all went on their way," Police Sgt. Lowell Hoffman said.

Mrs. Roy Marion, whose residence at 10797 Osgood was firebombed around 5:35 a.m.

today, told firemen she had been beaten up in the fracas last night on Osgood.

The house at 10724 San Jose, where firemen were summoned to treat victims of the second fight, was firebombed around 2:35 a.m. today.

The Fire Department Rescue crew treated fight victims at 10724 San Jose, but only Bell went to the hospital, with the other victim, a male, saying he didn't want to go to the hospital, Fire Department Capt. Howard Horton said.

Hoffman said Bell, who lives on a different street in Lynwood, told them he didn't know why he was attacked. Hoffman said Bell suffered a three-and-a-half inch cut on the forehead, stab wounds in the left shoulder area of the back and the mid back, and a three inch cut on his left forearm.

Possibility that the incidents may have been gang-related is being investigated he said. "We are trying to determine why this occurred and who was involved."

Horton said two molotov cocktails were thrown at the San Jose house, with one landing on the front porch and the other going into a front plate glass window into the dining room and causing an estimated $400 to $500 damage.

Police Jail Mom, Son As Fire Bombers In Burning On Osgood

Six people, including a mother and son, have been jailed by police on charges of fire bombing a house at 10 797 Osgood last Friday morning but are still searching for those believed resp onsible for a similar incident at 10724 San Jose. Booked on suspicion of arson and conspiracy to commit arson are David Paul Woodard, 19, of 10724 San Jose; John Hall Williams, 18, of 10726 Barlow; Richard Dean Olson, 18, of 7781 Fernwood; Villa Marie Acorn, 41, of 3875 Imperial Highway; her son, Steven Russell Acorn, 20, of 11036 Long Beach Boulevard; and a 17-year-old girl.

Police said the Osgood fire bombing occurred after the incident on San Jose and was believed to have been in retaliation. Officers are still searching for those involved in the first fire bombing.

The San Jose fire bombing occurred at 2:30 a.m. at the home of Nora Johanson, 50. This is also the home of David Woodard. A fire in the dining room caused extensive damage when a Molotov Cocktail smashed through the bay window. Second fire was started on the front porch when another Molotov Cocktail landed there.

Mrs. Johanson said she was asleep when she was awakened by the fumes.

The second fire bombing, for which the arrests were made, occurred at 5:25 a.m.

Police said some of the suspects had been involved earlier in two fights — one of which occurred at 10729 Osgood and the other at 10714 San Jose.

Injured in one of the fights was Lawrence Andrew Bell, 19, of 10726 Barlow. He was taken to St. Francis Hospital for emergency treatment of stab wounds and tire iron-inflicted injuries.

152

Mom Freed, Son Held In Fire Bombing

A 41-year-old Lynwood woman was freed last week by police who said no charges were filed against her in the fire bombing of a house at 10797 Osgood. The woman was identified as Villa Maria Acorn of 3875 Imperial Highway. Her son, Steven Russell Acorn, 20, of 11036 Long Beach Boulevard, was, however, arraigned in Compton Municipal Court on charges of arson of an inhabited dwelling and manufacturing an explosive device.

Also freed, with no charges filed against them, were David Paul Woodard, 19, of 10724 San Jose, and a 17-year-old Long Beach girl.

Arraigned in municipal court — in addition to Acorn — were John Hall Williams, 18, of 10726 Barlow; Jackie Lynn Brueger, 18, of 11036 Long Beach Boulevard; and Richard Dean Olson, 18, of 2701 Fernwood Avenue.

Acorn, Williams, Brueger and Olson are charged with arson in the Molotov Cocktail bombing of the Osgood home. This is believed to be in retaliation of a similar incident at the Woodard home on San Jose. Police said no one is in custody on the fire bombing at the San Jose address.

'Tried to take gun' after L.B. chase
Man wrestling officer killed

**By Russ MacDonald
and Stan Leppard**
Staff Writers

A 20-year-old Long Beach man was shot and killed Monday when he tried to wrest a gun away from a policeman after a shooting chase, police said.

Frank Miller, of 1722 Lemon Ave., was killed instantly when the officer's gun discharged during the struggle on the Long Beach Freeway at 3 a.m., according to investigators.

Police said the chase started at 2:50 a.m. when a California Highway Patrol officer on the freeway at Third Street alerted the dispatcher that he was in pursuit of a stolen car and asked for assistance.

A Long Beach unit manned by Officers Jerry Gadbaw and L. Morgan joined the chase at Pacific Coast Highway and proceeded northbound on the freeway at speeds up to 85 miles per hour.

As the fleeing car neared Bandini Boulevard in the Bell area, the driver leaned out and "started firing at them with a rifle, the two Long Beach officers said.

The officers returned the fire, shattering the rear window of the fleeing vehicle. The driver pulled to a stop along the freeway and sat in the car with his hands up as the two officers approached with drawn guns.

As Gadbaw and Morgan opened the car door to pull the man out, he suddenly grabbed Gadbaw's pistol and tried to take it away, the officers said. The gun discharged and the bullet struck Miller in the head.

A police investigation is continuing.

Car Theft Suspect Slain After High-Speed Chase
Tried to Grab Officer's Revolver at End of 20-Mile Pursuit, Long Beach Police Say

A 20-year-old auto theft suspect was shot and killed by a Long Beach police officer early Monday after a 20-mile, high-speed chase on the Long Beach Freeway.

The suspect was identified as Frank Miller of 1722 Lemon Ave., Long Beach, who authorities later reported apparently had been driving his girlfriend's car without her permission.

Long Beach police Sgt. Robert Luman said Miller was shot in the head by officer Jarold Gadbaw when the suspect attempted to grab the officer's .38-caliber service revolver as the patrolman was pulling Miller from the car.

The incident began near the Long Beach Freeway at 3rd St. in Long Beach about 3 a.m. when Miller's girlfriend, whom authorities declined to name, flagged down a California Highway Patrol unit to report that Miller had stolen her car.

The woman, who had been following Miller in another car, gave officers a description of the fleeing vehicle and they set out in pursuit.

Several blocks north, at Pacific Coast Highway, Long Beach officers Gadbaw and Lebron Morgan pulled in behind the speeding Miller after hearing a radio report of a CHP pursuit involving a stolen car.

During the chase north, often at speeds of 85 m.p.h. Miller fired several shots from a .22-caliber semiautomatic rifle, police said, but none of the shots struck the pursuing patrol unit.

As the Long Beach cruiser drew near, Morgan fired a shotgun blast, shattering the rear window of Miller's vehicle, and the suspect pulled to a stop on the freeway shoulder near Bandini Blvd. in Bell moments later, police said.

Police said Gadbaw attempted to pull Miller from the car after the suspect lowered his hands as the officer approached the vehicle. The fatal shot was fired as the two men struggled near the car, police said.

Morgan, who had difficulty getting out of the patrol car because the door had jammed, was not involved in the struggle or shooting, police said.

Illinois Jurist Dies

BAL HARBOUR, Fla. (UPI)—Illinois Supreme Court Justice James A. Dooley, 63, director of the International Academy of Trial Lawyers, died at his winter home Sunday.

Dooley's wife said he had not been ill and the cause of death had not been determined. She said funeral arrangements will be made today.

154

Officer kills driver after long chase

A Long Beach man was shot and killed this morning during a scuffle with a Long Beach Police officer on the Long Beach Freeway just south of Bandini Avenue following a high speed car chase.

A California Highway Patrol car was pursuing a car driven by Frank Miller, 20, of Long Beach when a Long Beach Police car joined in the chase.

According to police, Miller fired several shots from a rifle at the officers. Long Beach police returned the fire and shot out Miller's car rear window.

Miller then pulled over to the side of the freeway. He put his hands in the air and remained in the vehicle.

As officers approached the car, Miller put his hands down. A Long Beach officer opened the driver's door and attempted to pull Miller out of the car.

A fight ensued, and Miller attempted to disarm the officer. The weapon discharged and struck Miller once in the head.

Newpaper from Liberia, Africa (2008)

Dad, my brother, Steven, and me

My brother, Steven, and me

When life was perfect in the eyes of a child

On the road heading to the Wild, Wild West

A 12-year-old child on the run

Me, 15 years old

Mom, my niece, Tawnya, and me

Mom and Frank

Mom

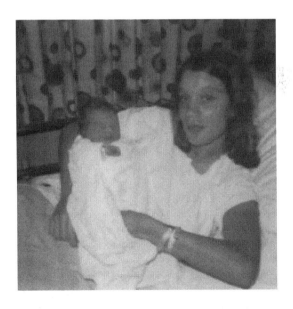

Lisa and me (November 15, 1977)

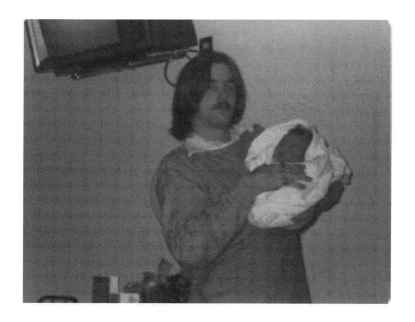

Frank and Lisa on her birthday

Lisa, Frank, and me—home from the hospital

Mom and Dad (Christmas 1977)

Frank and Steven

The three day binger (February 1978)

First picture after Frank's death

Gena, Steven, me (age 18), Dad, and Mom

Russia (1993)

I said "Yes!" (1993)

Dreams Really Do Come True

My beautiful niece, Rebekah Acorn

Emma, our Cystic Fibrosis warrior (left)
Emma and me (right)

Mom, some of the kids and grandkids, and me

Kevin and me

Kevin, Levi, Hope, and me

Lifelong friends: Reggie and me

Our family: Levi, Lisa (Emma's mom), me, Amy, Hope, Joshua and Kevin (seated)

The Be Finally Free Team

Be Finally Free Program Participants

Praise for
Freeing the Prisoner From Within
and
Debbie Ormonde

"Being the firstborn of a single mother—one who grew up in a life of chaos, poverty, addiction, and mental destruction—contributed to countless childhood adventures and lessons. I have watched my mother transform into a successful businesswoman and, more important, the woman God created her to be. Though she's endured heartbreak beyond your wildest imagination, by God's amazing grace, she is now walking in the fullness of His plan for her life. She is a living example that surrendering to Christ leads to complete freedom.

She has taught me the importance of being brave, the wisdom of listening to God, and the determination to achieve greatness. She took all of who she was, is, and will be, and poured it into my life. I am a better mom, wife, friend, and Child of God because of her and I am so proud that she is telling her life story—the good, bad, and ugly—in this book so that countless others can be as inspired by her as I am."

—Lisa Ritter
Debbie Ormonde's oldest daughter

"Debbie has been an active, faithful religious volunteer here at the Lerdo Detention Facility for many years, working with The Mission (a rehabilitation outreach) and helping me interview potential candidates for placement in The Mission recovery programs. She also ministers at the Crossroads Juvenile Facility, as well as other institutions.

Debbie's winsome, charismatic personality enables her to interact effectively with people from all walks of life. She has a natural ability to carefully navigate her way through life's various situations with wisdom and grace. Noting her passion for everything she does, people sense Debbie's sincerity and concern for those in need. Others love being around her because she is so upbeat and elevates the name of Jesus wherever she goes.

A very humble servant of the Lord, Debbie is working diligently to help establish a recovery home for women in a rural mountain community. She is very honest and forthright, and her integrity is beyond reproach.

Thank you, Debbie for showing the love of Jesus to the staff and inmates here at Lerdo and around the globe."

—Mike Franey
Chaplain, Lerdo Detention Facility

"Debbie is honest, dedicated, fearless, determined, compassionate, a bit crazy, focused, discerning, faithful, daring, funny, engaging, prayerful, determined, committed, visioned, humble, bold, resourceful, respectful, edgy, reachable, teachable, caring, old-school, Gospel-centered, and passionate—just to name a few things. You get what you see with her. There's no pretense, no faking it, and certainly no B.S.

Debbie has been through the fire and the rain, through the valleys and over the hills, through the desserts and up the rivers, and still she presses on. Why? Because of God!

Debbie is far from perfect, but she clings to the One who is: her

Savior and King … Lord and Provider … Beginning and End.

She is a true prayer warrior and I will stand with her and heartily endorse what God has given her to write in this book."

—Rev. Angelo Frazier
Pastor, RiverLakes Community Church

"I first met Debbie Ormonde in January of 2015 at Lerdo Detention Facility, where I now serve as Lead Chaplain. At Lerdo, I coordinate and schedule our 60 religious volunteers who conduct more than 20 religious services per week, including Bible studies, Celebrate Recovery meetings, and church services. On most weeks, Debbie is here on Mondays, Wednesdays, and Fridays. In addition, she consistently steps in to lead services and studies when additional volunteer coverage is needed.

As founder of Be Finally Free, her work in the community provides a great opportunity for paroling inmates to break the cycle of incarceration by attending classes, increasing their interview/job search skills, and, ultimately, finding meaningful employment. She provides crucial encouragement to maintain active involvement in their church.

Given her background, professional experience, education, and (above all) her passion and sincere heart to reach out to 'the least of these' in our society, Debbie is an invaluable asset to Lerdo's Chaplain Services and to the community as a whole. I have often said (only half-jokingly) that we could have 60 volunteers at Lerdo, or 3 Debbie Ormondes!"

—Mike Pitocco
Lead Chaplain, Lerdo Detention Facility

"After relocating the Be Finally Free (BFF) headquarters to our church facility, Debbie's team has been instrumental in encouraging men and women to become assets to our community through numerous classes. We have heard personal testimonies from many who were released from Lerdo Detention Facility and who are endeavoring to change their home lives, obtain work, and pursue clean living through BFF's positive reinforcement, love, and guidance. Many have told me that this much-needed encouragement began at Lerdo through BFF classes and teaching.

It is rare to find an organization that has such a heart for prisoners, not expecting any reward except to see changed lives. Pastoring for the past 30 years, I find it gratifying to see an association so dedicated to the rehabilitation of inmates."

—**Charles Lack**

Senior Pastor, Vessels of Honor Ministries

"After watching Debbie come to Lerdo Detention Facility day after day and week after week with her unmistakable passion, and watching the response of the inmates and personnel alike, I began to understand the difference that one seriously motivated individual can make here. Not just to appease the inmates or just get them through, but to offer hope of real change. She is truly an amazing sold-out soldier for Christ.

Debbie is making a real difference, not only here at Lerdo, but throughout the entire community and everywhere she goes. In fact, I was so excited about her and what she is doing, that I went with her to the Mission (where many of our inmates go for rehab). She has a lot of excellent ammunition in her ministry arsenal, such as parenting classes, GED preparation, counseling, and much, much more. She is meeting spiritual and practical needs, and offering hope and restoration to a lost and dying world."

—**Tracy Hale**

Chaplain, Lerdo Detention Facility

"I first met Debbie when she was 12 years old and I was 16. She was the most unusual young girl I've ever met. Debbie's childhood was anything but normal. Her story shows how the human spirit can be torn and broken; but, in finding God's love and acceptance, lives can be changed, repaired, and used to inspire others. God's greatest soldiers are the people who have been challenged, fallen down, trampled on, and still get up to face another day. Debbie's journey has been a long, hard road, but she trusted in God to get her through it all and she is an inspiration to every life she touches."

—Ann Maskill

President, Main Street Insurance Company

Rochester, Michigan